Kingdom
Encounters

The staff and students of

Ridley Hall CAMBRIDGE

CANTERBURY
PRESS
Norwich

© Ridley Hall 2009

First published in 2009 by the Canterbury Press Norwich
Editorial office
13–17 Long Lane,
London, EC1A 9PN, UK

Canterbury Press is an imprint of Hymns Ancient and Modern Ltd
(a registered charity)
St Mary's Works, St Mary's Plain,
Norwich, NR3 3BH, UK

www.scm-canterburypress.co.uk

British Library Cataloguing in Publication data

A catalogue record for this book is available
from the British Library

978 1 84825 001 7

Printed and bound in Great Britain by
CPI Bookmarque, Croydon

Contents

Preface

Last year, in *The Cast of the Kingdom,* we explored individual characters in the Bible and ways in which we can learn from them as we follow Christ. The imitation of the lives of other Christians is deeply rooted in our faith: Paul himself urged members of the Corinthian church to 'follow my example, as I follow the example of Christ' (1 Corinthians 11.1).

It seems apt to turn the spotlight away from individuals this year, and onto some of the many ways in which the people of God have been changed by meeting one another. In chance encounters (is anything ever chance with God?), in planned meetings; in homes, sacred buildings and on the road; through interruptions by angels, by friends and foes and God himself, God's mission unfolds throughout the Scriptures as people come together with each other, and with him.

It is hardly surprising that God should work his purposes out through such encounters. We are most fully human when we are two or three gathered together: this is how God made us, and he made us in his image and likeness. Furthermore, when people meet, we learn more about the nature of God than through any individual. The mutual love that Father, Son and Holy Spirit have for one another is the blueprint for all community. The early church was convinced that the three strangers who visited Abraham and Sarah (Genesis 18) were God himself; many Christians still read it in this way. Drawing on this, the great Russian icon-painter Michael Rublev gave us the immortal image of the three persons of the Trinity in table fellowship, inviting us to participate in the heavenly banquet.

So each of the readings and reflections in this book contains an encounter. In some, God is centre-stage, while others are very earthy, human, sometimes sinful engagements. But in every one, we know that God is at work, moulding, shaping, guiding, healing. Here is the story of how God works with people on the way, revealing himself to them and to us.

For the first time, this Ridley Hall collection of meditations comes from The Simeon Centre for Prayer and the Spiritual Life, one of the Hall's 'bridges out' initiatives in sharing resources with the Church in these islands and further afield. It fitted the Centre's aims very well, and we were glad to act as midwives for the project. As ever, the reflections came from students, staff and spouses at Ridley Hall writing during Lent 2009.

We offer this book to you as part of your Christian journey, on your own or in a group. Members of the Simeon Community and friends of the Centre will be praying for you and all who read it, and we would love to have feedback from you in due course, about things that have struck you: testimonies of the goodness and guidance of God as you have shared in these encounters through the Holy Spirit's inspiration.

Again, we are grateful to Christine Smith and the Canterbury Press for working with us tirelessly and sympathetically with this book. The proceeds from it will go to further the work of God's Kingdom through the mission and ministry of Ridley Hall, an Anglican theological college based in Cambridge, England. This year, the University of Cambridge celebrates its 800th anniversary, and we dedicate the book to the continuance of sound and godly Christian learning in that institution, founded for this specific purpose in 1209.

For more information about Ridley Hall and the Simeon Centre, please see the last pages of this book.

Using this Book

In a group

Ridley Hall's Lent meditations have proved to be excellent 'starters' for small group discussion. The experience of many groups has been that simply talking about how the prior week's reflections have spoken to group members has been enough to generate conversations and prompt insights that have been highly valued. These have, in turn, built confidence and mutuality, sometimes to an unexpected degree. Perhaps this is because the meditations derive from the wide-ranging life experiences of Ridley's students, and so easily provoke empathy and establish common ground with the readers.

As an individual

- Each day during Lent, set aside some time in a quiet place. You will need only this book, as the relevant Bible passages accompany each reflection.
- Do whatever helps you to relax – sit somewhere quiet, make a drink, take some deep breaths.
- Pray for God's Spirit to guide you before you read.
- Read the Bible passage set for the day – slowly – and think about what it might be saying.
- Then read the reflection for the day – again slowly – and pause for thought as you go. How does it relate to the Bible passage? Is there anything in the reflection which is similar to or different from anything you have experienced or thought before?
- When you have read and reflected, pray about what you have read and ask God what he might be saying to you through it; you might like to use the Lord's Prayer to finish.

The Daily Reflections

Matthew 4.1−4

Then Jesus was led by the Spirit into the wilderness to be tempted by the devil. After fasting forty days and forty nights, he was hungry. The tempter came to him and said, 'If you are the Son of God, tell these stones to become bread.'

Jesus answered, 'It is written: "People do not live on bread alone, but on every word that comes from the mouth of God."'

Jesus and Satan: Making Choices

Jesus' journey into the desert was a descent into hell. On the road for forty days and nights 'with wild animals', dried out by the heat and desperately hungry, he had only his Father's commendation to hold on to: 'This is my Son, whom I love; with him I am well pleased.' I have to remind myself, however, that a sense of purpose and mission doesn't make the desert feel any less bleak. Jesus' first encounter after his baptism was a meeting with the Devil.

Strange though it seems, this encounter is a missionary meeting. Not that Jesus attempts to convert Satan. That is not his task. But in his chastisement of the tempter, his words sound a challenge and an encouragement to us all: we may not descend into hell, but as we journey into a careless and broken world, we come face to face with the same temptations.

The challenge is this: we go into our own deserts to carry out the mission of our gracious redeeming God. On the way, we have many attractive encounters, often seemingly innocuous. As disciples, nothing, not even harmless life-giving bread, may distract us from doing our Father's will. The encouragement is that in our struggles with temptation, 'we have one who has been tempted in every way, just as we are', who understands, sympathizes and helps us in our weakness.

Lord Jesus Christ, Son of the living God, you went into the desert to wrestle not only Satan, but your own will. Give me grace that, in you, I too may wrestle, and win, for the sake of your Father's Kingdom. Amen.

Matthew 4.5–7

Then the devil took him to the holy city and had him stand on the highest point of the temple. 'If you are the Son of God,' he said, 'throw yourself down. For it is written:

"He will command his angels concerning you,
  and they will lift you up in their hands,
  so that you will not strike your foot against a stone."'

Jesus answered him, 'It is also written: "Do not put the Lord your God to the test."'

Jesus and Satan: Weapons of Warfare

What was it about Jesus that enabled him to stand against Satan with such confidence?

His main weapon was his security in God. He knew who he was, and did not need to prove himself to the enemy. He knew he was God's Son, and did not need to throw himself off a building to prove it. We see this time and again in Jesus' ministry, right to the end. As he hung on the cross, his opponents challenged him to come down – if he indeed was the Son of God. But Jesus knew his purpose, and trusted God's plans. He had nothing to prove.

In the same way, our main weapon must be our security in God. We have nothing to prove; trying to prove ourselves will only lead us away from God's perfect peace. It will lead, in short, to defeat.

True to his character, the father of all lies tried to use Scripture to trick Jesus, just as he twisted God's words to trick Eve and Adam in Eden. His traps are often subtle – what could be wrong with quoting Scripture? This is Jesus' second weapon: he was rooted in the fullness of God's Word. We too must know the Word well enough to understand when it is being taken out of context, and when it is used in a way that doesn't honour the message of the Bible as a whole.

Dear Lord, thank you so much for your Son, and for all I have to learn from his time on earth. Thank you that you have equipped me with all I need for a life of godliness. Help me to know your Word better, and to have an unshakeable faith in who you are, and your glorious plans for my life. Amen.

Matthew 4.8-11

Again, the devil took him to a very high mountain and showed him all the kingdoms of the world and their splendour. 'All this I will give you,' he said, 'if you will bow down and worship me.'

Jesus said to him, 'Away from me, Satan! For it is written: "Worship the Lord your God, and serve him only."'

Then the devil left him, and angels came and attended him.

Jesus and Satan: Counterfeit Worship

Jesus' third encounter with the Devil concerns the heart of religious life: worship. The Devil attempts to entice Jesus with an offer he can't refuse – all the power in the world coupled with a lavish lifestyle for a simple exchange: that Jesus bow down and worship him. A tempting offer, but Jesus will not be misguided.

He will not be misguided about *who* to worship: worship must be directed to God and God alone. Not the Devil, nor any human being or institution; God alone is to be worshipped.

Nor will Jesus be misguided as to *what* worship is. According to the Devil, worship is a means to an end, an exchange for something in return. But Jesus offers nothing in exchange. Worshipping God is not a transaction: there is no *quid pro quo* when it comes to Jesus. Instead we're simply asked to serve.

This may seem pretty straightforward, but it's easier than we think for our worship to be misguided. It can be all too tempting to treat worship as an opportunity, a time to get something in return: an uplifting religious experience or 'all our problems washed away'. Or we may find ourselves focussing less on God and more on what we do. This is not, however, the kind of worship Jesus is talking about. Worship is not about us but about God. It is a self-sacrificial response to the self-sacrificial love of God, characterized not by what we can get out of it, but by who God is.

Dear Lord, help me to recognize those times when my worship of you becomes misguided in any way. Teach me to worship you alone, to give you my life in deep thankfulness and to serve you because of who you are, for in this alone will I find true peace. Amen.

Genesis 4.3–10

In the course of time Cain brought some of the fruits of the soil as an offering to the LORD. But Abel also brought an offering—fat portions from some of the firstborn of his flock. The LORD looked with favour on Abel and his offering, but on Cain and his offering he did not look with favour. So Cain was very angry, and his face was downcast.

Then the LORD said to Cain, 'Why are you angry? Why is your face downcast? If you do what is right, will you not be accepted? But if you do not do what is right, sin is crouching at your door; it desires to have you, but you must rule over it.'

Now Cain said to his brother Abel, 'Let's go out to the field.' While they were in the field, Cain attacked his brother Abel and killed him.

Then the LORD said to Cain, 'Where is your brother Abel?'

'I don't know,' he replied. 'Am I my brother's keeper?'

The LORD said, 'What have you done? Listen! Your brother's blood cries out to me from the ground.'

Cain and God: Second Chances

Did you ever notice that God gave Cain a second chance?

Cain's offering to God gives a first glimpse of the progress of sin after the Fall, how it corrupts thoughts and actions, always 'crouching at the door'. For while Abel made his offering in faith, Cain wore a mask of piety that quickly slipped, and revealed the anger and envy that lurked in his heart.

Yet God spoke to Cain. In mercy he condescended to help Cain turn from his wickedness and rule over his sin rather than letting it rule over him. Cain encountered a *patient* God, and so do we – a God who reveals to us our shortcomings only to help us grow.

Cain rejected this 'second chance'; anger and envy festered in his life and led to murder. The brevity of the description suggests the callousness with which Cain killed his brother. And yet again God confronted Cain in mercy, not anger, giving him the chance to confess and repent. But Cain once more rejected God, even lied to him. God gives us second and third (and sometimes more) chances, but if we persist in turning from him, then we have no excuse.

As we look towards the cross, let us rejoice that the blood of Christ speaks a better word than the blood of Abel! For Jesus' blood cried out for forgiveness, and by *his* wounds we are healed.

Heavenly Father, I rejoice that you give me chance after chance, as you did your child Cain. Give me the grace to welcome all these second chances in my life, and help me to make them count. Amen.

Matthew 1.18–25

This is how the birth of Jesus the Messiah came about: His mother Mary was pledged to be married to Joseph, but before they came together, she was found to be pregnant through the Holy Spirit. Because Joseph her husband was a righteous man and did not want to expose her to public disgrace, he had in mind to divorce her quietly.

But after he had considered this, an angel of the Lord appeared to him in a dream and said, 'Joseph son of David, do not be afraid to take Mary home as your wife, because what is conceived in her is from the Holy Spirit. She will give birth to a son, and you are to give him the name Jesus, because he will save his people from their sins.'

All this took place to fulfil what the Lord had said through the prophet: 'The virgin will conceive and give birth to a son, and they will call him Immanuel' (which means 'God with us').

When Joseph woke up, he did what the angel of the Lord had commanded him and took Mary home as his wife. But he had no union with her until she gave birth to a son. And he gave him the name Jesus.

Joseph and the Angel: A Righteous Man

Joseph followed the Jewish law scrupulously, and truly loved God, hence his description: 'a righteous man'.

Joseph's righteousness acted out at these crossroads: he would have presumed Mary had been unfaithful, but he had mercy on her and did what was right. His intention was to divorce her quietly and not make trouble for her. Then, on meeting the angel, he obeyed God in the most extraordinary way and decided to marry Mary as God commanded, trusting she would give birth to Jesus – the one who saves people from their sins! Amazing!

This is the challenge to us: obey God! It may be that he won't send us an angel, but he has left us with something even better, his Word, the Bible. The Bible isn't just a history book; it is the living speaking word of a living speaking God. By obeying his Word, we display some of the same characteristics as Joseph.

When I read all of this, I am encouraged to stand firm in what God has called me to; to trust that what God has planned is far better than anything the world can offer. Joseph trusted God when he stood by Mary. People would have thought he was crazy for standing by a woman who claimed she was pregnant but still a virgin. Joseph knew what God had told him to do and he stood firm in that. Let us do the same.

Dear Lord Jesus, help me to know your plan for my life more and more. Help me today and every day to stand firm in what you have called me to. Use me to be a light in the darkness for the sake of your glory. Amen.

Genesis 12.10–20

Now there was a famine in the land, and Abram went down to Egypt to live there for a while because the famine was severe. As he was about to enter Egypt, he said to his wife Sarai, 'I know what a beautiful woman you are. When the Egyptians see you, they will say, "This is his wife." Then they will kill me but will let you live. Say you are my sister, so that I will be treated well for your sake and my life will be spared because of you.'

When Abram came to Egypt, the Egyptians saw that Sarai was a very beautiful woman. And when Pharaoh's officials saw her, they praised her to Pharaoh, and she was taken into his palace. He treated Abram well for her sake, and Abram acquired sheep and cattle, male and female donkeys, male and female servants, and camels.

But the LORD inflicted serious diseases on Pharaoh and his household because of Abram's wife Sarai. So Pharaoh summoned Abram. 'What have you done to me?' he said. 'Why didn't you tell me she was your wife? Why did you say, "She is my sister", so that I took her to be my wife? Now then, here is your wife. Take her and go!' Then Pharaoh gave orders about Abram to his men, and they sent him on his way, with his wife and everything he had.

Abram and Sarai in Egypt: Acting in Fear

I find this encounter in Abram's long life quite offensive. He's at least seventy-five years old, and has moved from Ur to Canaan in obedience to the Lord's call. Times become hard, and he and Sarai move to Egypt.

He's clearly terrified, panicking about his new neighbours, fearing for his own skin. At the border post, he confides in Sarai and invites her to lie, 'so that I will be treated well for your sake'. Sarai complies and is taken into Pharaoh's household, whereupon disease breaks out.

Pharaoh is punished; Sarai becomes a slave-woman for a while. Abraham gets off scot-free. Pharaoh acts as a real gentleman towards him, whereas my response would have been brutal. How dare he exploit his wife and his new masters so cavalierly?

But then I find myself strangely convicted by this story. How many times have I also turned truth into a lie to my own advantage, exploited the situation to make the most of it for myself? I wonder what the consequences have been for the others – often the silent others – in the story of my selfishness.

So at the end I'm left with all sorts of theological questions, and a personal challenge. I have set out on my journey in obedience to the call of God. Will I now trust God enough in the unfolding circumstances to care for me and mine, or will I like Abram try to bend the world to my will, in case God lets me down?

God of Abram and Sarai, forgive me for the times when I have paved my journey with deceit and half-truths. Guide me in the way of trust and righteousness, for your mercy's sake. Amen.

Matthew 8.5–13

When Jesus had entered Capernaum, a centurion came to him, asking for help. 'Lord,' he said, 'my servant lies at home paralyzed, suffering terribly.'

Jesus said to him, 'Shall I come and heal him?'

The centurion replied, 'Lord, I do not deserve to have you come under my roof. But just say the word, and my servant will be healed. For I myself am a man under authority, with soldiers under me. I tell this one, "Go," and he goes; and that one, "Come," and he comes. I say to my servant, "Do this," and he does it.'

When Jesus heard this, he was amazed and said to those following him, 'Truly I tell you, I have not found anyone in Israel with such great faith. I say to you that many will come from the east and the west, and will take their places at the feast with Abraham, Isaac and Jacob in the kingdom of heaven. But the subjects of the kingdom will be thrown outside, into the darkness, where there will be weeping and gnashing of teeth.'

Then Jesus said to the centurion, 'Go! Let it be done just as you believed it would.' And his servant was healed at that very hour.

Jesus and the Centurion: 'Say the word'

'Shall I come and heal him?' Jesus asked. If the centurion had answered 'yes', the healing of his servant would have been just like all those other healings that surround this story. Indeed, it seems that Jesus was expecting a 'yes', and would willingly have obliged. This time, however, it is not Jesus who shatters the expectations of the crowd but the centurion as he turns the tables with a boldness that astonishes even Jesus.

'Lord . . . just say the word . . . ' Living in the hierarchy of the army, the centurion knew how to speak to those in authority. He knew that to believe that Jesus was Lord was to believe that he had power: to believe that he could achieve results, without fail, every time.

As well as surprise at the centurion's boldness, perhaps Jesus' astonishment arose partly from seeing that this man knew, like few others, what it meant to call him 'Lord'. Drawing on his own experience of being one in authority, the centurion knew that a Lord who lacked authority was no Lord at all.

Faced with the authority that Jesus has, the centurion also displayed a remarkable humility. It is not a humility that denies who he is or the position that he holds amongst his own soldiers. Instead it is a humility that recognizes the presence of a Lord who has a greater authority and wields power that changes lives and can heal even from afar.

Lord of all creation, whose authority and power extends over all people, all places and all circumstances, I pray that you will grant me the boldness and humility to bring my needs before you. Just say the word. Amen.

Genesis 18.9–15

'Where is your wife Sarah?' they asked him.

'There, in the tent,' he said.

Then the LORD said, 'I will surely return to you about this time next year, and Sarah your wife will have a son.'

Now Sarah was listening at the entrance to the tent, which was behind him. Abraham and Sarah were already very old, and Sarah was past the age of childbearing. So Sarah laughed to herself as she thought, 'After I am worn out and my lord is old, will I now have this pleasure?'

Then the LORD said to Abraham, 'Why did Sarah laugh and say, "Will I really have a child, now that I am old?" Is anything too hard for the LORD? I will return to you at the appointed time next year and Sarah will have a son.'

Sarah was afraid, so she lied and said, 'I did not laugh.' But he said, 'Yes, you did laugh.'

Sarah and Abraham: Accepting the Impossible

Long ago God had promised Abraham more descendants than he could count, along with the land that they would need. But God seems to have been acting slowly, and up until now the only way that Abraham has got an heir is by subversion, impregnating the slave girl Hagar at the insistence of his infertile wife. This isn't God's plan.

Sarah doesn't believe she will ever bear children, and by human standards that's not an unreasonable assumption. She's now ninety and has long ago given up hope. Yet when the angels bring the news that she's been waiting all her life to hear she can't accept it and laughs out loud. Here is real confirmation: God has already told Abraham that the new son will be called Isaac, 'he laughs'.

Often I get an idea during prayer and, wanting to see immediate results, I try to project my own plan onto it. But if I act too fast, I end up doing what I want to do in my own strength, not what God wants me to do in his, and I fail. I've often had to accept that I can't do everything I'd like to get involved with – there simply isn't time – so I'm gradually learning to slow down, to prayerfully consider things, to discern which things are for now, and which are for another time and another place.

God can do anything. We just need to let him do it, according to his plan, not ours.

Lord, help me to listen to you, and to rely not on my own strength but yours. With you, the impossible comes true. Without you, the truth is impossible. Amen.

Matthew 11.2–10

When John heard in prison what the Messiah was doing, he sent his disciples to ask him, 'Are you the one who was to come, or should we expect someone else?'

Jesus replied, 'Go back and report to John what you hear and see: The blind receive sight, the lame walk, those who have leprosy are cleansed, the deaf hear, the dead are raised, and the good news is proclaimed to the poor. Blessed is anyone who does not stumble on account of me.'

As John's disciples were leaving, Jesus began to speak to the crowd about John: 'What did you go out into the wilderness to see? A reed swayed by the wind? If not, what did you go out to see? A man dressed in fine clothes? No, those who wear fine clothes are in kings' palaces. Then what did you go out to see? A prophet? Yes, I tell you, and more than a prophet. This is the one about whom it is written:

"I will send my messenger ahead of you,
  who will prepare your way before you."'

Jesus and John the Baptist: Dealing with Doubt

John was convinced that the time had come for God to visit his people. His role had been to preach the message: 'Get right with God or face the consequences!' He had been sure that Jesus was the One. But where was the judgement that the prophets had said would accompany God's appearing? His confinement in what was probably a sunless rocky cave beneath Herod's palace gave him plenty of time to ponder whether or not he might have been mistaken.

Like John, we also can find ourselves confused and disturbed by experiences that contradict our expectations. John was expecting a radical clean-up operation, but I know (having stood in that dim cave myself), that his experience would have given the impression that he was the one being cleaned up! Suffering and injustice disturb us: when we are the victims it is easy to imagine that God has stopped caring.

But, like John, we need Jesus' gentle reminder of the bigger picture. I imagine John might have initially been more than a little bemused by Jesus' answer. Jesus simply reaffirms what he's been doing, which John already knows. It's this that provoked his doubt in the first place! But a reflection on Jesus' phrasing would have reminded John of Isaiah 35 and 61. God's appearing would involve salvation and release as well as judgement. The Scriptures show us, as they showed John, that Jesus is the One and that unfulfilled expectations are not a cause to stumble but an invitation to review and increase our faith.

Lord Jesus, when doubts overwhelm me and things don't go as expected, please remind me that you still sit on the throne. Help me to keep trusting you and not to look elsewhere. Amen.

Genesis 22.1–8

Some time later God tested Abraham. He said to him, 'Abraham!' 'Here I am,' he replied.

Then God said, 'Take your son, your only son, whom you love—Isaac—and go to the region of Moriah. Sacrifice him there as a burnt offering on a mountain I will show you.'

Early the next morning Abraham got up and loaded his donkey. He took with him two of his servants and his son Isaac. When he had cut enough wood for the burnt offering, he set out for the place God had told him about. On the third day Abraham looked up and saw the place in the distance. He said to his servants, 'Stay here with the donkey while I and the boy go over there. We will worship and then we will come back to you.'

Abraham took the wood for the burnt offering and placed it on his son Isaac, and he himself carried the fire and the knife. As the two of them went on together, Isaac spoke up and said to his father Abraham, 'Father?' 'Yes, my son?' Abraham replied. 'The fire and wood are here,' Isaac said, 'but where is the lamb for the burnt offering?'

Abraham answered, 'God himself will provide the lamb for the burnt offering, my son.' And the two of them went on together.

Abraham and Isaac: 'What if?'

What would have happened if . . . ? Why did this have to happen . . . ? Just think what might have happened . . . ! We ask 'what if' questions every day: they are part of what it means to be human.

Here on the mountain, despite Isaac's one question, we are given, not an account of 'what if', but a story of what did happen. God sets up, on a journey, a test of obedience that beggars belief. Abraham obeys and sets out. By the end, we have been taken far beyond anything we could have imagined, and witness a blessing that sets Abraham, Isaac and their descendants apart for all time.

Like Abraham, how we respond to the incomprehensible challenges of life largely depends on how we view God. Abraham's reaction came out of his experience and knowledge of God and can be found in the verse, 'God himself will provide.' There is no 'what if' thinking in Abraham's response, just a strong belief in the faithfulness and goodness of God.

Obeying God's call can end up like living on a knife edge if the 'what if' questions are allowed to consume our minds. But our story, like Abraham's, does not need to be strewn with 'what ifs'. Abraham had faith in God's unfailing faithfulness, and so can we. Faithfully believing in God's goodness enables us to trust that 'God will provide' all we need for the journey and destination, wherever that may be.

Merciful and most loving Father, I praise you for your unending faithfulness. By your grace may I grow deeper in faith this day, learn to say 'Yes' to you and plumb the depths of your sustaining love on my journey. Amen.

Matthew 15.21–28

Leaving that place, Jesus withdrew to the region of Tyre and Sidon. A Canaanite woman from that vicinity came to him, crying out, 'Lord, Son of David, have mercy on me! My daughter is demon-possessed and suffering terribly.'

Jesus did not answer a word. So his disciples came to him and urged him, 'Send her away, for she keeps crying out after us.'

He answered, 'I was sent only to the lost sheep of Israel.'

The woman came and knelt before him. 'Lord, help me!' she said.

He replied, 'It is not right to take the children's bread and toss it to the dogs.'

'Yes it is, Lord,' she said. 'Even the dogs eat the crumbs that fall from their master's table.'

Then Jesus said to her, 'Woman, you have great faith! Your request is granted.' And her daughter was healed from that very hour.

The Canaanite Woman: Persevering Prayer

This woman was desperate. Her daughter was grievously sick and no one could help her. But one day Jesus came to her village. He'd never been before. Indeed it was very surprising that he was here now in foreign territory, but he needed a break from the endless probing of the scribes and the Pharisees. Rumours of his gifts as a healer had spread even here and she wasn't going to miss her opportunity.

The situation didn't look hopeful. Matthew describes her as a Canaanite, the word used of the pagan peoples who inhabited the Promised Land before the coming of the Israelites. In the normal course of events she wouldn't have expected Jesus to engage with her. But she is desperate. She shouts at Jesus, begging for mercy; Jesus ignores her. Perhaps that is what she expected.

But she won't give up, and even when Jesus tells her that he has come only for the Jews, she refuses to be put off. She knows Jesus can heal her daughter, she knows that nothing about her circumstances deserves to receive Jesus' blessing, but isn't that what grace is all about? And her perseverance is rewarded.

This woman is a challenge to me. She makes me see how quickly I give up if it seems that my requests have not been heard. She shows me that I can argue with Jesus, that he seemed to relish a robust exchange. She reminds me of Jesus' words to his disciples in Luke 18.1 about their need 'to pray always and not to lose heart'.

Lord Jesus, keep me faithful in prayer, and when I am tempted to give up, teach me never to lose heart. Amen.

Genesis 39.6–12

So Potiphar left everything he had in Joseph's care; with Joseph in charge, he did not concern himself with anything except the food he ate.

Now Joseph was well-built and handsome, and after a while his master's wife took notice of Joseph and said, 'Come to bed with me!'

But he refused. 'With me in charge,' he told her, 'my master does not concern himself with anything in the house; everything he owns he has entrusted to my care. No one is greater in this house than I am. My master has withheld nothing from me except you, because you are his wife. How then could I do such a wicked thing and sin against God?' And though she spoke to Joseph day after day, he refused to go to bed with her or even be with her.

One day he went into the house to attend to his duties, and none of the household servants was inside. She caught him by his cloak and said, 'Come to bed with me!' But he left his cloak in her hand and ran out of the house.

Joseph and Potiphar's Wife: Facing Demons

Even at this point in his career, there are early signs of the political wisdom that would take Joseph on to a role of leadership in Egypt. As he responds to Potiphar's wife, Joseph resists her demands and, in doing so, displays an unquestioning obedience to God.

We are told that it was Joseph's physical appearance that attracted Potiphar's wife to the young Israelite. What we don't know is whether Joseph shared that attraction, because he does not answer her with reference to his own desires. Instead, he invokes his responsibility both to Potiphar and to God. Tempted he may have been, but his goal is to please God alone.

Joseph's response would be echoed hundreds of years later when Jesus faced the Devil's temptations. We don't know with what desire Jesus saw the riches of the world laid out in front of him, but we do know that he overcame those temptations by calling on the name of the one whom he served: 'Away from me, Satan! For it is written: "Worship the Lord your God, and serve him only."'

There is no coincidence in the way in which first Joseph and then Jesus 'faced their demons'. One thing that we can be sure of is that we will all have our demons to face. How we face them is up to us. If our relationship with God is more important to us than our desire to please ourselves, then however weak we feel we will be able to tackle any temptations in God's strength, and win.

Father God, be the one who is always in my sight. Walk before me, around me and beside me. Thank you that, in your strength, I can face down any temptations. Amen.

Mark 5.21–34

When Jesus had again crossed over by boat to the other side of the lake, a large crowd gathered around him while he was by the lake. Then one of the synagogue leaders, named Jairus, came, and when he saw Jesus, he fell at his feet. He pleaded earnestly with him, 'My little daughter is dying. Please come and put your hands on her so that she will be healed and live.' So Jesus went with him.

A large crowd followed and pressed around him. And a woman was there who had been subject to bleeding for twelve years. She had suffered a great deal under the care of many doctors and had spent all she had, yet instead of getting better she grew worse. When she heard about Jesus, she came up behind him in the crowd and touched his cloak, because she thought, 'If I just touch his clothes, I will be healed.' Immediately her bleeding stopped and she felt in her body that she was freed from her suffering.

At once Jesus realized that power had gone out from him. He turned around in the crowd and asked, 'Who touched my clothes?'

'You see the people crowding against you,' his disciples answered, 'and yet you can ask, "Who touched me?"'

But Jesus kept looking around to see who had done it. Then the woman, knowing what had happened to her, came and fell at his feet and, trembling with fear, told him the whole truth. He said to her, 'Daughter, your faith has healed you. Go in peace and be freed from your suffering.'

A Ruler and an Outcast: Two Meetings, One Outcome

Two people, so different from each other and both so needy: a ruler of the synagogue, male, powerful and respected; a woman, second class, powerless, untouchable, rejected because of her condition. Both were desperate: Jairus' beloved daughter was going to die, the doctors no more able to save her than they were able to cure the woman who had spent all her money consulting them.

Both meetings with Jesus are last – ditch attempts: Jairus and the unnamed woman were willing to try anything, to believe anything in the remote chance that it might help. But although they were both desperate, each came with absolute faith and confidence. Jairus didn't ask Jesus if he could heal his daughter. Instead, he said, 'if you lay hands on her she will live'. At the last possible moment – and after the 'interruption' by the haemorrhaging woman, Jesus confounded the mockers, reassured Jairus, went in with him to face the worst, and restored his daughter to life.

The woman knew that if only she touched Jesus' clothes she would be healed. And so it was: Jesus healed her physically, but, in acknowledging her, healed her socially too, restoring her to the community.

Their faith inspires us not only to believe, but to act in the light of that belief. We too can have confidence that Jesus will respond to us in our times of greatest need.

Thank you, Lord Jesus, that I can come to you in times of desperation, with confidence and faith. I know that you will not ignore me or reject me, but will acknowledge me and walk with me, giving me the strength to face hard times with you alongside me. Amen.

Numbers 22.27–31

When the donkey saw the angel of the LORD, it lay down under Balaam, and he was angry and beat it with his staff. Then the LORD opened the donkey's mouth, and it said to Balaam, 'What have I done to you to make you beat me these three times?'

Balaam answered the donkey, 'You have made a fool of me! If only I had a sword in my hand, I would kill you right now.'

The donkey said to Balaam, 'Am I not your own donkey, which you have always ridden, to this day? Have I been in the habit of doing this to you?'

'No,' he said.

Then the LORD opened Balaam's eyes, and he saw the angel of the LORD standing in the road with his sword drawn. So he bowed low and fell face down.

Balaam, the Angel, and the Donkey: How God Gets Our Attention

There are various ways to get someone's attention, but normally a polite 'Excuse me' or a tap on the shoulder will suffice. If this, or perhaps a yell, does not work, we might be tempted to use firmer methods! The Lord God, too, is not averse to using shock tactics to bring us to our senses.

When the Israelites were journeying towards the Promised Land, the Moabite king asked the prophet Balaam to curse them. After quelling his misgivings, Balaam headed off, perched on his faithful donkey. Reaching a narrow point in the road, the donkey came to a halt, refusing to budge. Balaam was livid. Finally, as he took his stick to her, she opened her mouth and spoke.

This didn't faze Balaam one bit, and he replied angrily. Only then were his eyes opened to see the angel of the Lord blocking the way. In a trice, he fell prostrate and listened. The Lord had finally grabbed Balaam's attention. The angelic message counters Balaam's original commission with interesting consequences: to find out more, read on.

The unexpected in God's encounters with us is often his way of seizing our attention in order to guide us. I have no experience of talking donkeys, I've only ever heard them whinny, but accidentally overhearing a throwaway comment about myself changed the direction of my life. I was stunned to hear my spiritually sceptical father say what he did to an uncle at a family gathering, and at last I was ready to hear what God had to say.

Lord, keep my ears and eyes open so that I may never miss the ways in which you seek to get my attention. Amen.

Mark 10.17–22

As Jesus started on his way, a man ran up to him and fell on his knees before him. 'Good teacher,' he asked, 'what must I do to inherit eternal life?'

'Why do you call me good?' Jesus answered. 'No one is good—except God alone. You know the commandments: "You shall not murder, you shall not commit adultery, you shall not steal, you shall not give false testimony, you shall not defraud, honour your father and mother."'

'Teacher,' he declared, 'all these I have kept since I was a boy.'

Jesus looked at him and loved him. 'One thing you lack,' he said. 'Go, sell everything you have and give to the poor, and you will have treasure in heaven. Then come, follow me.'

At this the man's face fell. He went away sad, because he had great wealth.

The Rich Young Man: Stripped Bare

In a world where we are surrounded by so many opportunities to consume, this passage is a huge challenge. It is one that I have found difficult in the past, holding on to my possessions and the things I valued for dear life. There is something alarming about Jesus implying that we should give away all that we have. However, as life moves on we find ourselves facing situations through which we are changed and our faith deepened.

Nothing has been quite so profound for me as when my mother was diagnosed with terminal cancer and given less than six months to live. As I sat with her day after day, I looked around the room at all her possessions. Suddenly it hit me how futile they all were. What was she to do with them? They were absolutely no use to her now.

As she approached death, my mother's faith was solid and steadfast. Jesus Christ was all that she needed and the simplicity of it was quite beautiful.

This passage echoes Jesus' teaching in the Beatitudes. Jesus makes it clear that it is only when we are stripped bare of everything that we have that we are truly blessed. This does not mean that God wants us to suffer, but his deepest desire for us is that we learn that his grace is sufficient: we can and we must completely depend on him.

Father God, thank you for the difficult and challenging experiences of life. Help me to depend on you every day, because you are everything that I need. Amen.

Joshua 2.8–14

Before the spies lay down for the night, she went up on the roof and said to them, 'I know that the LORD has given this land to you and that a great fear of you has fallen on us, so that all who live in this country are melting in fear because of you. We have heard how the LORD dried up the water of the Red Sea for you when you came out of Egypt, and what you did to Sihon and Og, the two kings of the Amorites east of the Jordan, whom you completely destroyed. When we heard of it, our hearts melted in fear and everyone's courage failed because of you, for the LORD your God is God in heaven above and on the earth below.'

'Now then, please swear to me by the LORD that you will show kindness to my family, because I have shown kindness to you. Give me a sure sign that you will spare the lives of my father and mother, my brothers and sisters, and all who belong to them—and that you will save us from death.'

'Our lives for your lives!' the men assured her. 'If you don't tell what we are doing, we will treat you kindly and faithfully when the LORD gives us the land.'

Rahab and the Spies: Hearing, Believing, Acting

I've always called myself Christian. I grew up in a Christian home and attended a church school. I heard about Jesus and learned the Lord's Prayer alongside my ABC. I believed in him and I trusted in him, but it was a very simple belief.

I've often regretted the 'wasted' years when I thought that my faith was too simple to count. Yet Rahab's rooftop encounter with the Israelite spies shows how powerful a simple belief can be.

Here was a woman who lived on the edge of Jericho society both morally and physically, relying on that society for her very survival. Yet she hid two strangers who posed a great danger, and lied to her king in order to save them. She betrayed her people, putting herself and her family at risk. Why?

In this encounter, the 'why' becomes clear: she had heard about God and, having heard, she believed. We're told that all of Jericho believed. Their fear of God meant that they expected Israel's eventual victory – a sharp contrast to forgetful Israel's own understanding of God's sovereignty. For Rahab, though, belief led to action.

Rahab's later, deepening, faith was to catapult her into Jesus' genealogy as his direct ancestor (Matthew 1.5). Yet it was her early simple belief – a belief born of hearing rumours of God – that was both her immediate salvation and Israel's passport into the Promised Land.

Out of the simplest faith, we can choose between God's authority and the world's, and he will use us mightily for his purposes. Are we ready to act on the faith we have?

Almighty God, I have heard of your great love for the world, the 'rumours' of good news. Work in me, I pray, to turn my hearing into belief and my belief into action. Amen.

Luke 1.18–30

Zechariah asked the angel, 'How can I be sure of this? I am an old man and my wife is well on in years.'

The angel said to him, 'I am Gabriel. I stand in the presence of God, and I have been sent to speak to you and to tell you this good news. And now you will be silent and not able to speak until the day this happens, because you did not believe my words, which will come true at their appointed time.'

Meanwhile, the people were waiting for Zechariah and wondering why he stayed so long in the temple. When he came out, he could not speak to them. They realized he had seen a vision in the temple, for he kept making signs to them but remained unable to speak.

When his time of service was completed, he returned home. After this his wife Elizabeth became pregnant and for five months remained in seclusion. 'The Lord has done this for me,' she said. 'In these days he has shown his favour and taken away my disgrace among the people.'

In the sixth month of Elizabeth's pregnancy, God sent the angel Gabriel to Nazareth, a town in Galilee, to a virgin pledged to be married to a man named Joseph, a descendant of David. The virgin's name was Mary. The angel went to her and said, 'Greetings, you who are highly favoured! The Lord is with you.' Mary was greatly troubled at his words and wondered what kind of greeting this might be. But the angel said to her, 'Do not be afraid, Mary, you have found favour with God.'

Zechariah's Angel: God has not Forgotten

God often seems to have chosen older men and women to fulfil his purposes. This sometimes included the gift of a child in very old age. Retirement is not on God's agenda: for some, it is when they are well advanced in years that God begins to unfold the most important aspects of his plan.

Zechariah was a case in point: his very name means 'God has remembered'. He was chosen by lot to enter the holy place of the Temple to burn fragrant incense in worship. Zechariah had a prayer lying heavily on his heart as he longed for the gift of a child. Perhaps, as he looked at the golden lampstand with its almond flowers and buds, he was reminded how often things begin with a bud and then blossom into God's possibilities. Yet when Zechariah saw the angel by the altar of incense assuring him that his prayer had been heard and would be answered, he doubted.

When we hold a prayer in our hearts, God may have planted it there; his plan may be bigger than our limited vision. God proved himself to be a gracious giver, showing favour to an elderly couple whose doubt was finally silenced by his powerful Word. They not only rejoiced in the birth of their own son, but shortly afterwards in the miraculous birth of the Messiah and Saviour of the whole world, the one whose way was prepared by the son of their old age.

Faithful God, help me never to lose heart, to trust you to fulfil your promise and your will in my life, and to work with you till the end of my days. Amen.

Ruth 1.11–12 and 15–18

But Naomi said, 'Return home, my daughters. Why would you come with me? Am I going to have any more sons, who could become your husbands? Return home, my daughters; I am too old to have another husband. Even if I thought there was still hope for me—even if I had a husband tonight and then gave birth to sons . . .

'Look,' said Naomi, 'your sister-in-law is going back to her people and her gods. Go back with her.'

But Ruth replied, 'Don't urge me to leave you or to turn back from you. Where you go I will go, and where you stay I will stay. Your people will be my people and your God my God. Where you die I will die, and there I will be buried. May the LORD deal with me, be it ever so severely, if even death separates you and me.' When Naomi realized that Ruth was determined to go with her, she stopped urging her.

Ruth, Naomi, Orpah: Total Commitment

Whenever I read Ruth's words to Naomi I am amazed and humbled. All worldly logic and common sense is on Naomi's side, when she urges her two Moabite daughters-in-law to return to their families. She herself has no husband, no property, no future. Obediently Orpah kisses Naomi and returns home, and we expect Ruth to do the same.

Far from it! Ruth 'clings to her', and with an astonishing oath makes a decision of unfathomable courage. Today we deal in conditionals and provisos, in small print and pre-nuptial agreements, in hedging bets and spreading risks. Ruth, though, holds nothing back, 'till death us do part'. It is only through this complete commitment that she discovers the blessing of the God she has glimpsed in Naomi. It is a blessing that finally gives her far more than they could have ever asked for or imagined.

Ruth's words are sometimes used in marriage services, but they are even truer of our baptismal vows. As Christians we, like Ruth, choose to follow a path that is marked by death, symbolized by a cross. Again and again I look with envy at other paths that appear easier and less risky. Ours may be a path marked by death but Ruth shows us that it is also a path that leads to life. Only as we commit ourselves wholly to the crucified Christ can we discover the risen Christ. Only as we walk the way of the cross can we uncover (in good time) the blessing of God, who gives life in all its fullness to those who entrust everything to him.

Lord of life and death, help me to love you with all of my heart and soul and might, so that I may know the joy of the risen Christ. Amen.

Luke 1.39–45

At that time Mary got ready and hurried to a town in the hill country of Judea, where she entered Zechariah's home and greeted Elizabeth. When Elizabeth heard Mary's greeting, the baby leaped in her womb, and Elizabeth was filled with the Holy Spirit. In a loud voice she exclaimed: 'Blessed are you among women, and blessed is the child you will bear! But why am I so favoured, that the mother of my Lord should come to me? As soon as the sound of your greeting reached my ears, the baby in my womb leaped for joy. Blessed is she who has believed that the Lord would fulfil his promises to her!'

Elizabeth and Mary: Rivals or Partners?

Why are Christmas round robin letters filled with parents' lengthy accounts of the achievements of their children? One may be forgiven for suspecting a hint of one-upmanship that was probably never intended.

In two different parts of Palestine two cousins, the older in the south and the younger in the north, were each surprised by the news brought by angelic messengers. Each was to be gifted with a son and each had a husband who found it hard to believe the angel's promise. Each of their sons was to be special and play a unique part in God's plan to bring salvation and forgiveness of sins to a troubled people in a sin-filled world.

Yet there was no hint of one-upmanship when Mary and Elizabeth finally met. The older woman's baby leapt in her womb, recognizing the one for whom he would pave the way with his preaching. Elizabeth praised God for the greater blessing given to her cousin who would be mother to God's own son. They were united in faith, united in blessing, united in their 'yes' to God's summons. Not many years later they would be united in their sorrow, after they had lost their sons to cruel and violent deaths.

What a challenge to rejoice in God's gifts and to hear and respond to God's plan for my life, however humble it may appear compared to his plan for others. There is a challenge too to recognize that there is a cost for all God's servants in saying 'yes' to his summons.

Dear Lord, give me the same spirit of unity and partnership that Mary and Elizabeth had. Help me also to say 'Yes' to you without hesitation and without condition. Amen.

1 Samuel 1.12–20

As she kept on praying to the LORD, Eli observed her mouth. Hannah was praying in her heart, and her lips were moving but her voice was not heard. Eli thought she was drunk and said to her, 'How long will you keep on getting drunk? Get rid of your wine.'

'Not so, my lord,' Hannah replied, 'I am a woman who is deeply troubled. I have not been drinking wine or beer; I was pouring out my soul to the LORD. Do not take your servant for a wicked woman; I have been praying here out of my great anguish and grief.'

Eli answered, 'Go in peace, and may the God of Israel grant you what you have asked of him.'

She said, 'May your servant find favour in your eyes.' Then she went her way and ate something, and her face was no longer downcast.

Early the next morning they arose and worshiped before the LORD and then went back to their home at Ramah. Elkanah lay with Hannah his wife, and the LORD remembered her. So in the course of time Hannah conceived and gave birth to a son. She named him Samuel, saying, 'Because I asked the LORD for him.'

Hannah and Eli: What You See is What You Get?

Well, that's how the expression goes, but it's rarely that simple. How often do we get the wrong end of the stick and make judgements about other people that are simply untrue? That's exactly what Eli did in this story.

The first time I read it I was struck by the intimacy of Hannah's prayer. Her relationship with the Lord was such that she could acknowledge fully the pain and sorrow of her childlessness; her supplication is deeply moving in its sincerity. As I pondered on it, however, my focus shifted to Eli, the priest. He had observed her praying silently. He saw her lips moving and assumed she was drunk. He simply got it wrong, but God didn't allow Eli's impaired judgement to get in the way. God's agenda is more important. So then Eli listens, to her and no doubt to God, and he is touched by what he hears. He blesses her, asking that God answers her prayer and, indeed, he does!

I'd love to say that it is Hannah, the deeply prayerful woman of the story that I relate to, and it is, in the sense that I hope that I can be as honest in what I ask for, and as free with my thanksgiving as she was. However, I think it is Eli, the man who makes the mistake, who resonates with me. I hope that when I am out of order, opening my mouth before I have the true picture, that God will also right my wrongs and enable me to see him at work.

Heavenly Father, thank you that I can always have confidence in you, and that you are present even when I get it wrong. I pray that you will help me to learn from my mistakes and give me the chance to put them right. Amen.

Luke 7.44–50

Then he turned toward the woman and said to Simon, 'Do you see this woman? I came into your house. You did not give me any water for my feet, but she wet my feet with her tears and wiped them with her hair. You did not give me a kiss, but this woman, from the time I entered, has not stopped kissing my feet. You did not put oil on my head, but she has poured perfume on my feet. Therefore, I tell you, her many sins have been forgiven—as her great love has shown. But whoever has been forgiven little loves little.'

Then Jesus said to her, 'Your sins are forgiven.'

The other guests began to say among themselves, 'Who is this who even forgives sins?'

Jesus said to the woman, 'Your faith has saved you; go in peace.'

Jesus, Simon and a Nameless Woman: Actions Speak Louder than Words

They certainly do: this is Jesus' message to an aloof, unwelcoming and judgemental Simon. The woman, on the other hand, not only accorded Jesus the usual greetings. She washed his feet with tears, dried them with her hair and extravagantly anointed his feet with ointment.

All this was, as Jesus knew, an act of deep repentance; all she felt and knew to be true about herself and Jesus was reflected in her loving actions. At no time are we told that she *said* anything.

Jesus asked Simon 'Do you see this woman?' Maybe he was asking Simon to see her as he, Jesus, saw her, to observe 'the outward and visible signs of the inward and invisible grace' that was being bestowed on her at that moment, irrespective of her behaviour in the past. Simon was witnessing a vital part of Jesus' ministry: the transformative power of forgiveness.

Why is this so important for me? It is because I know for myself the dramatic effect of forgiveness so freely given by God. I want Jesus' power to continue changing me, transforming my relationships with others. I'd like to set aside my human cynicism and self-righteousness (the 'Simon' in me), and truly see the individual in front of me as someone created by God in his likeness; someone capable of having that image restored through the transforming power of Jesus' love and forgiveness. And Jesus shows me the way.

Lord, you know everything there is to know about each one of us, and nothing is beyond the power of your forgiveness and all-embracing love. Help me to be true to you and allow you to transform my life. Amen.

1 Samuel 17.43–47

He said to David, 'Am I a dog, that you come at me with sticks?' And the Philistine cursed David by his gods. 'Come here,' he said, 'and I'll give your flesh to the birds and the wild animals!'

David said to the Philistine, 'You come against me with sword and spear and javelin, but I come against you in the name of the LORD Almighty, the God of the armies of Israel, whom you have defied. This day the LORD will deliver you into my hands, and I'll strike you down and cut off your head. This very day I will give the carcasses of the Philistine army to the birds and the wild animals, and the whole world will know that there is a God in Israel. All those gathered here will know that it is not by sword or spear that the LORD saves; for the battle is the LORD's, and he will give all of you into our hands.'

David and Goliath: In Whose Strength?

I love the story of David and Goliath. It is one of the earliest Old Testament stories that I can remember being read to me as a child. The frightening, towering figure of Goliath, brought down by the small shepherd boy with a sling, then beheaded with his own sword.

We join the story during a strong exchange of words between the two characters. Both project supreme confidence – one in weapons and worldly strength, the other in God's name. Goliath says he'll give David's flesh to the birds of the air and the beasts in the field, to which David replies that, unlike Goliath's trust in a sword and javelin, he comes in the name of the Lord.

David is as confident in the name of the Lord as Goliath is in his mighty sword and javelin. The challenge for us is: do we have that same confidence in the name of the Lord? As David says, the battle is the Lord's and he will defeat his enemies. It is the small stone from David's sling that provides the lethal blow to Goliath's forehead. The name of the Lord might seem similarly small, but it is mighty and powerful. Like David, we need to trust and call on his name to win our battles, and not rest on our own strength.

Thank you, Lord, that I do not need to rely on a sword or my own strength, but that I can call on your name every day to help me in each battle that I face. Amen.

Luke 19.1–10

Jesus entered Jericho and was passing through. A man was there by the name of Zacchaeus; he was a chief tax collector and was wealthy. He wanted to see who Jesus was, but because he was short he could not see over the crowd. So he ran ahead and climbed a sycamore-fig tree to see him, since Jesus was coming that way.

When Jesus reached the spot, he looked up and said to him, 'Zacchaeus, come down immediately. I must stay at your house today.' So he came down at once and welcomed him gladly.

All the people saw this and began to mutter, 'He has gone to be the guest of a sinner.'

But Zacchaeus stood up and said to the Lord, 'Look, Lord! Here and now I give half of my possessions to the poor, and if I have cheated anybody out of anything, I will pay back four times the amount.'

Jesus said to him, 'Today salvation has come to this house, because this man, too, is a son of Abraham. For the Son of Man came to seek and to save what was lost.'

Zacchaeus and Jesus: A Sinner Comes Home

Throughout Scripture, we encounter characters whose stories are bound up in the meaning of their names. Peter is 'the Rock'; Daniel means 'God is my judge'; Mary is 'beloved'. Zacchaeus' name implies that he is 'clean'. Yet when we first meet him, the tax collector seems anything but. Money-focused, betraying his own people by collecting taxes for the Romans, he was despised and detested by the people of Jericho.

When Jesus invited himself to stay at Zacchaeus' house, he knew what the reaction would be. Eating with a tax collector was a violation of the accepted norms: Jesus had transgressed the social and religious boundary that separated the 'clean' from the 'unclean'. What was he doing?

Unlike the crowd and even the tax collector himself, Jesus knew who Zacchaeus really was. Reaching across the social divide, Jesus had extended grace and mercy to a sinner. And what an effect it had! Jesus' order carried enough force to make Zacchaeus immediately repent of his sins. Before Jesus even reached his house, Zacchaeus' life had changed radically. He could now begin to live in the freedom of his real name: he was now justifiably 'clean'.

Jesus invites each one of us, whoever we are and whatever our reputation is, to open our houses and our lives to him. Associating with Jesus is a special event; powerful and life-changing. All we have to do to accept his call is to open the doors of our hearts and welcome him in.

Lord Jesus, I welcome you into my heart and I ask you to cleanse my soul from selfishness and ungodliness. Amen.

1 Kings 17.10–15

So he went to Zarephath. When he came to the town gate, a widow was there gathering sticks. He called to her and asked, 'Would you bring me a little water in a jar so I may have a drink?' As she was going to get it, he called, 'And bring me, please, a piece of bread.'

'As surely as the LORD your God lives,' she replied, 'I don't have any bread—only a handful of flour in a jar and a little olive oil in a jug. I am gathering a few sticks to take home and make a meal for myself and my son, that we may eat it—and die.'

Elijah said to her, 'Don't be afraid. Go home and do as you have said. But first make a small loaf of bread for me from what you have and bring it to me, and then make something for yourself and your son. For this is what the LORD, the God of Israel, says: "The jar of flour will not be used up and the jug of oil will not run dry until the day the LORD sends rain on the land."'

She went away and did as Elijah had told her. So there was food every day for Elijah and for the woman and her family.

Elijah and the Widow of Zarephath: Gracious Sharing

I remember the first time I drove across a desert: thirteen hours of driving almost in a straight line across a featureless landscape strewn with the litter of sun-scorched trees. A breakdown would spell disaster, might lead to death. I was strangely comforted by the thought that the people of the desert would take me in, offer me water, bread and a bed. They had little, but in the culture of the desert they could survive. On the edge of survival themselves, they lived a life of sharing, of hospitality.

We sometimes read Elijah's story too quickly, jumping forward to the miracles. Elijah too was a man driving across a desert land of God's punishment. True, it is God who directed him to the widow of Zarephath. God knew that he could count on her hospitality, even at the end of her life.

She doesn't take much persuading. It may have been that she believed Elijah's prophetic words, that her heart leapt when she heard God's promise. The element of this encounter that strikes me most forcefully, however, is its underlying spirit of grace and generosity. Elijah is helpless in the desert and God graciously sends him to the widow. Her natural hospitality gives unstintingly, to the last grain of wheat and drop of oil. Through Elijah, her household is blessed by God and fed. The story culminates in resurrection, which is the outcome of grace.

Gracious God, you met the widow's needs through Elijah, and his needs through her. I am so grateful for your generosity towards me, and ask you to give me the same spirit of grace and generosity, that many may be blessed by you, through me. Amen.

John 2.1–5

On the third day a wedding took place at Cana in Galilee. Jesus' mother was there, and Jesus and his disciples had also been invited to the wedding. When the wine was gone, Jesus' mother said to him, 'They have no more wine.'

'Woman, why do you involve me?' Jesus replied. 'My hour has not yet come.'

His mother said to the servants, 'Do whatever he tells you.'

Jesus and Mary: A Gentle Push

For fans of the TV comedy shows of Harry Enfield and Paul Whitehouse, the sequence of events leading up to Jesus' very first miracle may seem uncomfortably familiar. When Mary prompts her son to step in to save the blushes of the groom when the wedding at Cana runs dry, Jesus initially rebuffs her in a manner not dissimilar to the refrain of surly teenager Kevin, 'You're so embarrassing . . .'

Far from mounting a display of adolescent rebellion, Jesus was sounding a subtle warning that the time was not right for his miraculous ministry to begin. But Mary had the confidence to persist, neatly side-stepping his refusal by advising the servants to be at his disposal. Jesus could quite easily have ignored her, but instead went on to perform the oft-wished-for miracle of turning water to wine, leading to cheers all round for the unknowing groom.

Mary's gentle promptings are akin to one of the ways in which God communicates with us: the still, silent voice. And the response of Jesus is a perfect example of how we should respond to God's direction in our lives – despite initially questioning Mary's direction, Jesus goes ahead and obeys, to the glory of the Father. The challenge we are left with is to have the ears to hear God's subtle guidance, and to be ready to act on it.

Lord God, give me the ears to hear your guidance today, and the boldness to follow your prompting. Amen.

1 Kings 18.25–30

Elijah said to the prophets of Baal, 'Choose one of the bulls and prepare it first, since there are so many of you. Call on the name of your god, but do not light the fire.' So they took the bull given them and prepared it.

Then they called on the name of Baal from morning till noon. 'Baal, answer us!' they shouted. But there was no response; no one answered. And they danced around the altar they had made.

At noon Elijah began to taunt them. 'Shout louder!' he said. 'Surely he is a god! Perhaps he is deep in thought, or busy, or travelling. Maybe he is sleeping and must be awakened.'

So they shouted louder and slashed themselves with swords and spears, as was their custom, until their blood flowed. Midday passed, and they continued their frantic prophesying until the time for the evening sacrifice. But there was no response, no one answered, no one paid attention.

Then Elijah said to all the people, 'Come here to me.' They came to him, and he repaired the altar of the LORD, which had been torn down.

Elijah and the Prophets of Ba'al: Solid Faith vs. Desperate Pleading

The big prize fight is announced. People discuss the contenders – weight, stamina, and power. Who will go the distance?

The people of God have, once again, turned their backs on him. Everywhere there are shrines to Ba'al and Asherah, and Elijah appears from nowhere and pronounces God's judgement of a drought for three years. Then he disappears for three years, only to reappear and announce a 'show down' between God and Ba'al. The contest would be hotly debated. Both God and Ba'al were said to speak through the thunder, and both were said to use fire from heaven as their weapon. Who would win?

Today it's hard to imagine the spectacle: Four hundred prophets of Ba'al, and one Elijah. Four hundred men jumping and shouting and slashing themselves with knives, their voices reaching a climax as they call on Ba'al to respond and prove his right to be worshipped. One Elijah sitting by, his taunting becoming increasingly sarcastic. Four hundred exhausted men, dumbfounded that their god had not responded, gathering to watch Elijah rebuild God's altar. Four hundred shocked men as God's fire from heaven destroys both the altar and its offering in response to Elijah's heartfelt prayer – and the crowd goes wild!

We live in an ever-changing world, and those who don't worship God seem sometimes to far outnumber those who do. Elijah's solid faith in God is a strong lesson. No matter what the odds, God is God. God alone is to be worshipped. God alone responds to prayer. God alone provides.

Father, may I have the faith to know that you alone are God. You alone are the one who hears and answers my prayers and provides for me no matter what the circumstances. Amen.

John 4.7–15

When a Samaritan woman came to draw water, Jesus said to her, 'Will you give me a drink?' (His disciples had gone into the town to buy food.)

The Samaritan woman said to him, 'You are a Jew and I am a Samaritan woman. How can you ask me for a drink?' (For Jews do not associate with Samaritans.)

Jesus answered her, 'If you knew the gift of God and who it is that asks you for a drink, you would have asked him and he would have given you living water.'

'Sir,' the woman said, 'you have nothing to draw with and the well is deep. Where can you get this living water? Are you greater than our father Jacob, who gave us the well and drank from it himself, as did also his sons and his flocks and herds?'

Jesus answered, 'Everyone who drinks this water will be thirsty again, but those who drink the water I give them will never thirst. Indeed, the water I give them will become in them a spring of water welling up to eternal life.'

The woman said to him, 'Sir, give me this water so that I won't get thirsty and have to keep coming here to draw water.'

The Samaritan Woman and Jesus: Liberating Boldness

Even at the best of times it's a risky business approaching strangers. How much more risky for the Samaritan woman? She has come to draw water at the hottest time of day. She has come as an outcast – friendless, alone, and despised. Normally, she might have expected to have the well to herself, but today there is a stranger there, not merely a man, but a Jew.

I sense her feelings of trepidation and despair at the thought that she might actually have to face this man. For her, it's not a case of 'if', but 'how', she will be abused. What will he say? Will she be forced to leave the well empty handed?

Her reaction to Jesus' first question might seem blunt. Is she shocked? Confused? I like to think that beneath it all there is an unacknowledged spark of hope that someone is willing to treat her as a normal human being.

In the conversation that follows, the thing I admire most about this woman is her boldness. Initially, she is not prepared to leave the well without her water, and then not without hearing what this 'prophet' has to say. However, once she realizes that Jesus is the 'Messiah' who will 'explain everything to us', her water jar is forgotten and her priority is to find those people she has previously tried so hard to avoid.

In a single meeting with Jesus this woman is set free, confident that she knows and is known by the living God. Her response? To share her freedom. Would I do the same in her position? Boldness to tell people about Jesus is one thing that I want more of. In God's grace, the woman was able to bring others to Jesus. May it be something we all have the joy of doing.

Father, set me free as you set the Samaritan woman free from her past life. Give me her boldness, joy and enthusiasm, so that those to whom I go may come to know, believe in and follow your Son. Amen.

2 Kings 2.9–14

When they had crossed, Elijah said to Elisha, 'Tell me, what can I do for you before I am taken from you?'

'Let me inherit a double portion of your spirit,' Elisha replied.

'You have asked a difficult thing,' Elijah said, 'yet if you see me when I am taken from you, it will be yours—otherwise, it will not.'

As they were walking along and talking together, suddenly a chariot of fire and horses of fire appeared and separated the two of them, and Elijah went up to heaven in a whirlwind. Elisha saw this and cried out, 'My father! My father! The chariots and horsemen of Israel!' And Elisha saw him no more. Then he took hold of his garment and tore it in two.

He picked up the cloak that had fallen from Elijah and went back and stood on the bank of the Jordan. Then he took the cloak that had fallen from him and struck the water with it. 'Where now is the LORD, the God of Elijah?' he asked. When he struck the water, it divided to the right and to the left, and he crossed over.

Elijah and Elisha: Faith and Devotion

Elijah's final moments on Earth are fittingly dramatic for one used to invoking fire on his enemies, or receiving food from ravens. But it is not the fireworks of the prophet's ascension to heaven – complete with whirlwind and fiery chariots and horses – that I find striking; rather it's the insistent devotion and great faith of his attendant, the God of Israel's anointed prophet-in-waiting, Elisha.

The apprentice had already fended off his master's attempts to uncermoniously ditch him on three occasions. Elisha's devotion duly proven beyond doubt, Elijah asked his protégé what he could do for him before leaving for the final time. Elisha immediately asked for a double portion of the spirit of his hugely spirit-filled master. Did he realize the scale of his request? Undoubtedly – it was a demonstration of his faith in God to equip him for the task that lay ahead of him, as God's messenger to a rebellious and fractious nation. Elijah agreed but decided to test the commitment of the young pretender one last time, setting the condition that he must be watching when the sweet chariot swung low.

I love the picture of blazing horses and chariots descending from heaven to carry Elijah home, as though God had laid on his finest cavalcade to collect his faithful servant. But the exit left Elisha distraught, despite having witnessed the whole spectacle, and it was not until he struck the Jordan with Elijah's cloak, symbolically passed on to signify God's anointing, that he discovered the Lord was still with him.

Heavenly Father, give me the faith to ask for more than I can hope for, the courage to receive your gifts, and the energy to act on your generosity as Elisha did. Amen.

John 9.24–34

A second time they summoned the man who had been blind. 'Give glory to God and tell the truth,' they said. 'We know this man is a sinner.'

He replied, 'Whether he is a sinner or not, I don't know. One thing I do know. I was blind but now I see!'

Then they asked him, 'What did he do to you? How did he open your eyes?'

He answered, 'I have told you already and you did not listen. Why do you want to hear it again? Do you want to become his disciples too?'

Then they hurled insults at him and said, 'You are this fellow's disciple! We are disciples of Moses! We know that God spoke to Moses, but as for this fellow, we don't even know where he comes from.'

The man answered, 'Now that is remarkable! You don't know where he comes from, yet he opened my eyes. We know that God does not listen to sinners. He listens to the godly person who does his will. Nobody has ever heard of opening the eyes of a man born blind. If this man were not from God, he could do nothing.'

To this they replied, 'You were steeped in sin at birth; how dare you lecture us!' And they threw him out.

A Blind Man and his Detractors: Giving Glory to God

'Give glory to God!' rings the command of the Pharisees – 'Tell it as it is.'

This man, born blind, told his story as it was. A social misfit shackled by disability and suspicion, he had encountered a man called Jesus and everything had changed forever. He hadn't worked it out yet, but he knew what he knew: no one could take *that* away from him.

This encounter put him on a collision course with the great and the good. He was left with two stark choices: either to bail out, tell them what they wanted to hear and be accepted; or tell it as it was and face rejection. For him, there was no contest. He, unlike the Pharisees, gave true glory to God.

For me, it's so often been different, and I confess my compromised choices with a heavy heart. For the cheap pay-off of respect, knowing full well that Jesus is my Saviour too, I retell my story without God in it, to save face, to avoid embarrassment, to make myself look good. This is the antithesis of 'Giving Glory to God'. This is the *theft* of Glory.

There is often a cost to telling the truth about our encounters with God, and it is certainly no longer politically correct to talk about meeting Jesus. Yet what an opportunity there is for us in a world as careless and as scornful as the blind man's was, to speak as he spoke, secure in the faith that no one can take from us what we have been given by Jesus: new, abundant, eternal life.

Heavenly Father, may I always have the courage to give you the glory, knowing your saving and healing grace. Save me from the temptation to protect myself from your detractors, and keep me telling the truth. Amen.

2 Chronicles 9.1−2, 5−8

When the queen of Sheba heard of Solomon's fame, she came to Jerusalem to test him with hard questions. Arriving with a very great caravan—with camels carrying spices, large quantities of gold, and precious stones—she came to Solomon and talked with him about all she had on her mind. Solomon answered all her questions; nothing was too hard for him to explain to her.

She said to the king, 'The report I heard in my own country about your achievements and your wisdom is true. But I did not believe what they said until I came and saw with my own eyes. Indeed, not even half the greatness of your wisdom was told me; you have far exceeded the report I heard. How happy your people must be! How happy your officials, who continually stand before you and hear your wisdom! Praise be to the LORD your God, who has delighted in you and placed you on his throne as king to rule for the LORD your God. Because of the love of your God for Israel and his desire to uphold them for ever, he has made you king over them, to maintain justice and righteousness.'

Solomon and the Queen of Sheba: Worthwhile Wisdom

How to get there? That must have been the first question. Jerusalem was hundreds of miles away, across the Arabian desert. Carried on a litter and fanned by servants, the queen of Sheba was spared the worst hardships of the dusty journey. Yet we can't underestimate the effort that she went to in her desire to see the famous Solomon.

Every jolting day of travel proved worthwhile. Solomon's God had blessed him abundantly. The queen's wealth was considerable, but the king's was greater still and his wisdom . . . Well, she tested him with question after question and found his answers true.

Sadly, even a queen couldn't stay for ever. Sheba needed her. So she left the fabulous city, the roof of its new temple glinting high above her, and its fortunate inhabitants still enjoying life in the wonderful land their God had given them. She returned home amazed and humbled at all she'd seen and heard. What she didn't know was that Solomon's reign marked the end of an era. The monarchy soon fell. Eventually temple and land would follow.

It would be nearly a thousand years before Israel's fortunes were properly restored, and then in a way that nobody – not even Solomon – could have imagined. The Gentile queen came, once, from the ends of the earth to hear Israel's king. Now, 'one greater than Solomon is here' (Matt. 12.42) and the Gentiles come again, to hear the wisdom of King Jesus. Listen! Can you hear his voice?

Father, give me the humility to sit at the feet of your Son, to hear his words of wisdom and to receive from him great blessing. Amen.

John 11.38–44

Jesus, once more deeply moved, came to the tomb. It was a cave with a stone laid across the entrance. 'Take away the stone,' he said. 'But, Lord,' said Martha, the sister of the dead man, 'by this time there is a bad odour, for he has been there four days.'

Then Jesus said, 'Did I not tell you that if you believe, you will see the glory of God?'

So they took away the stone. Then Jesus looked up and said, 'Father, I thank you that you have heard me. I knew that you always hear me, but I said this for the benefit of the people standing here, that they may believe that you sent me.'

When he had said this, Jesus called in a loud voice, 'Lazarus, come out!' The dead man came out, his hands and feet wrapped with strips of linen, and a cloth around his face. Jesus said to them, 'Take off the grave clothes and let him go.'

Jesus and Lazarus: No Barrier to Life

Last year I visited Israel. After spending time in the hubbub of Jerusalem's thriving commercial centre, our group took an excursion to Bethany – the setting for this story. Despite its proximity, Bethany is a 25-minute bus-ride: the original route from Jerusalem is blocked by the security wall dividing Israel and the West Bank. Eventually we arrived at a quiet, dusty side street inaccessible to buses. Opposite the church at Lazarus's tomb we found two little run-down shops and a couple of hawkers selling post cards.

This was the site of the last of Jesus' miraculous 'signs' that foreshadowed his own resurrection. Yet it seemed almost neglected and without easy access.

What specially struck me about Bethany was the impact of a wall erected on the direct route between the busy (and sometimes very religious) life of Jerusalem and the site where Jesus summoned forth life. I wonder how often I build a wall between myself and God, and become unaware of the signs of God's presence and power. How often do I make unnecessarily long journeys because of barriers that I have erected between myself and Jesus' summons to life?

What great resurrection stories might there be for each of us if we could navigate round, or even demolish, these road blocks, and find our way to the places where Jesus raises the dead? Where do you hear him calling you to dare to believe that he might do that for you today?

Lord Jesus, give me the insight to see the walls I have built between myself and your Kingdom, the courage to question them, and the power of your Holy Spirit to demolish them. Amen.

Esther 4.13–17

[Mordecai] sent back this answer: 'Do not think that because you are in the king's house you alone of all the Jews will escape. For if you remain silent at this time, relief and deliverance for the Jews will arise from another place, but you and your father's family will perish. And who knows but that you have come to royal position for such a time as this?'

Then Esther sent this reply to Mordecai: 'Go, gather together all the Jews who are in Susa, and fast for me. Do not eat or drink for three days, night or day. I and my attendants will fast as you do. When this is done, I will go to the king, even though it is against the law. And if I perish, I perish.'

So Mordecai went away and carried out all of Esther's instructions.

Esther and Mordecai: Stepping up to the Challenge

Esther's life since entering King Xerxes' palace had mostly been one of luxury, indulgence and privilege. While at times it may have been difficult – subservient to a volatile and fickle king, and having been plucked from obscurity to live in a palace far from those she loved – her life was one of comfort. Lavished with pampering sessions lasting for six months, she had people admiring her beauty and holding it in the highest esteem.

It doesn't seem far from the lives of modern-day celebrities, the people many see as role models – another young girl plucked from obscurity, as Kate Moss was at 14, and thrown into a lifestyle of privilege.

But this lifestyle turned out to be not all that God had planned for Esther. Her adopted father Mordecai uncovered a plot to persecute the Jews, so sought her help. Initially hesitant but compassionate to Mordecai's needs, Esther was scared to risk the wrath of the king. However, Mordecai asked her to do a much bigger thing – not just to care for his needs, but to rescue her people.

At the point that we join the story, Mordecai pushes her a step further, reminding Esther that the proclamation against the Jews would affect her, and that she might possibly be the only one who could prevent it. Indeed, this could be the very reason she was there. Esther rose to the challenge, risking far more than just her status as a beauty queen, to save the Jews and become a different kind of role model.

Heavenly Father, help me to stand up for the marginalized and persecuted, and by your strength, to play my part for your Kingdom in such a time as this. Amen.

Acts 3.1–10

One day Peter and John were going up to the temple at the time of prayer—at three in the afternoon. Now a man who was lame from birth was being carried to the temple gate called Beautiful, where he was put every day to beg from those going into the temple courts. When he saw Peter and John about to enter, he asked them for money. Peter looked straight at him, as did John. Then Peter said, 'Look at us!' So the man gave them his attention, expecting to get something from them.

Then Peter said, 'Silver or gold I do not have, but what I do have I give you. In the name of Jesus Christ of Nazareth, walk.' Taking him by the right hand, he helped him up, and instantly the man's feet and ankles became strong. He jumped to his feet and began to walk. Then he went with them into the temple courts, walking and jumping, and praising God. When all the people saw him walking and praising God, they recognized him as the same man who used to sit begging at the temple gate called Beautiful, and they were filled with wonder and amazement at what had happened to him.

Peter, John and the Lame Man: Time to Stop

Somewhere deep inside me is a Sunday clock that plays insistently 'Get me to the church on time.' It's really important. What does it say about me if I'm late? So imagine, there we are, my friend and I, on time, walking through town to the sound of the beckoning bells. People are coming from all around to pray and praise, entering through the lych gate into the churchyard and up the path to the church door. I won't be late. They'll all see me. On time. In my seat – ready to worship God.

But what's this, just inside the gate? A beggar? A 'down and out'? Looks as though he's crippled. Oh well, I'd love to stop . . . but God's waiting for me, you see, inside the church. With the nice people. Mustn't be late. What would they think? And anyway, there's not much I could do even if I stopped.

But there's another nagging voice within, crying 'Stop!' Jesus would, wouldn't he? I don't have much, but I could give my time, a smile, or maybe even a prayer. And then who knows, this poor man might even be healed. Where would that lead? I might even get to tell the crowd about it. The town might hear about what Jesus can do today, in the street, outside the church. Just because of '*a good deed done to someone who was sick*' on the way to church, at the time of prayer.

Lord, give me the courage to act on the impulse of your Holy Spirit. Free me from the conventions that imprison me, that I may respond faithfully to those who need my touch and yours. Amen.

Song of Solomon 3.1–5

All night long on my bed
I looked for the one my heart loves;
I looked for him but did not find him.
I will get up now and go about the city,
through its streets and squares;
I will search for the one my heart loves.
So I looked for him but did not find him.
The watchmen found me
as they made their rounds in the city.
'Have you seen the one my heart loves?'
Scarcely had I passed them
when I found the one my heart loves.
I held him and would not let him go
till I had brought him to my mother's house,
to the room of the one who conceived me.
Daughters of Jerusalem, I charge you
by the gazelles and by the does of the field:
Do not arouse or awaken love
until it so desires.

The Lover and the Beloved: Complete Fulfilment

Israel and her God, the Church and her Christ, the believer and his Saviour, or 'just' a simple love story? I like to think that it works for all of these relationships. It's the story of yearning for someone deeply loved, ending in the greatest of all encounters: the consummation of love.

I used to go on chaplaincy visits with my father to the docks when I was young. He would leave me in the car and go on board, telling me he wouldn't be longer than a few minutes. Sometimes, he was delayed, and I can remember my frantic, beating heart, longing to see him again, afraid that I would be left alone, not knowing how to get home, terrified of losing him.

There is a similar sense of breathlessness here, of the desperate lover, whose repetition reminds me of my own lurching fears: 'I looked . . . I looked . . . I will search . . . ' In the middle of the night, when decent people are in bed, she bumps into the night watchmen, and you can feel her grab them by their cloaks: 'Do you know where he is?' There is no shame, no self-consciousness: love unfulfilled takes over the whole of life. And when she finds him, she holds on for dear life, and takes him home, with a warning of the danger of all-consuming love.

In this universal poem, I am reminded of all my loves, my longing and its fulfilment. But at the heart of all my remembering, there is a deep ache: I yearn for a deeper, fuller, more passionate relationship no longer dependent on mood, need or circumstance. I long simply to be held by God.

You have made me for yourself, O Lord, and my heart is restless until it finds its rest in you. May I yearn for you with a yearning deeper than life itself and stronger than death, and in finding you, may I know true peace. Amen.

Acts 12.11–17

Then Peter came to himself and said, 'Now I know without a doubt that the Lord has sent his angel and rescued me from Herod's clutches and from everything the Jewish people were hoping would happen.'

When this had dawned on him, he went to the house of Mary the mother of John, also called Mark, where many people had gathered and were praying. Peter knocked at the outer entrance, and a servant named Rhoda came to answer the door. When she recognized Peter's voice, she was so overjoyed she ran back without opening it and exclaimed, 'Peter is at the door!'

'You're out of your mind,' they told her. When she kept insisting that it was so, they said, 'It must be his angel.'

But Peter kept on knocking, and when they opened the door and saw him, they were astonished. Peter motioned with his hand for them to be quiet and described how the Lord had brought him out of prison. 'Tell James and the other brothers and sisters about this,' he said, and then he left for another place.

Peter and Rhoda: Absolute Conviction

What a night it had been for Peter. Amidst the joyous turmoil of the early days of the church in Jerusalem, he found himself imprisoned as part of a crackdown by King Herod. James, brother of John, had already lost his life, and Peter probably owed his survival to the fact that Passover was still in progress. Herod had planned to parade him before the Jewish people once the festivities ended, the result of which can only be guessed at. Fortunately for Peter, not to mention the close huddle of believers who were keeping constant prayer for him, a mighty act of God saved the day.

Chained and asleep between two soldiers, Peter was woken by an angel but assumed he was experiencing a vision, only for the angel to release his chains and lead him out of the jail under the noses of the sleeping, or perhaps just unseeing, guards. Peter's first act after realizing he was free was to find his fellow believers, but he was hindered in this by the overjoyed response of Rhoda, the servant girl.

Rhoda's absolute conviction is an inspiration to me, and her fervent insistence that it was indeed Peter who stood outside in full bodily form – despite the slurs on her sanity from the other believers – is a great example of someone who turned conviction into immediate action. While the miraculous might not often occur in our daily lives, God still speaks to us in a host of ways, whether through prayer, Scripture or creation, during worship, or through the counsel of other Christians. Our challenge is to be like Rhoda and act with absolute conviction.

Father God, guide me by your Holy Spirit and convict me of the things that burden your precious son, Jesus Christ. Please give me the faith to act on those things about which you convict me today. Amen.

Daniel 3.14–20

Nebuchadnezzar said to them, 'Is it true, Shadrach, Meshach and Abednego, that you do not serve my gods or worship the image of gold I have set up? Now when you hear the sound of the horn, flute, zither, lyre, harp, pipe and all kinds of music, if you are ready to fall down and worship the image I made, very good. But if you do not worship it, you will be thrown immediately into a blazing furnace. Then what god will be able to rescue you from my hand?'

Shadrach, Meshach and Abednego replied to him, 'King Nebuchadnezzar, we do not need to defend ourselves before you in this matter. If the God we serve is able to deliver us, then he will deliver us from the blazing furnace and from Your Majesty's hand. But even if he does not, we want you to know, Your Majesty, that we will not serve your gods or worship the image of gold you have set up.'

Then Nebuchadnezzar was furious with Shadrach, Meshach and Abednego, and his attitude toward them changed. He ordered the furnace heated seven times hotter than usual and commanded some of the strongest soldiers in his army to tie up Shadrach, Meshach and Abednego and throw them into the blazing furnace.

Shadrach, Meshach, Abednego and Nebuchadnezzar: Faith Tested by Fire

How do we respond when our faith is tested? When we're faced with a decision to compromise our faith or risk alienation, ridicule or even physical harm?

Shadrach, Meshach and Abednego were faced with just this: a powerful king with a terrifying temper and a court order that directly violated the first commandment. It's far from being comfortable! Yet despite their circumstances these three Jewish boys were steadfast in their faith. History and their own experience had taught them that their God is a God who saved – and still saves. He can be trusted in this perilous situation.

But surely the most challenging part of the story is that these boys were still prepared to trust and obey God even if he had decided not to save them. Their faith was so certain and steadfast that they would rather be burned alive than worship something or someone other than the Most High God.

Whatever our circumstances, and whether or not God rescues us from our troubles, the Most High God is worthy of our undivided loyalty and worship, because of who he is and what he's already done for us. The cross and resurrection demonstrate that whatever situation we face, nothing can separate us from the love of God. The challenge we face is to remind ourselves of that fact when the world (or our own fear) tells us otherwise.

Lord, when I'm challenged to give my devotion and loyalty to things other than you, please help me to resist and not to compromise. For whatever happens to me, you have shown that you alone are worthy of my praise. Amen.

Acts 16.11–15

From Troas we put out to sea and sailed straight for Samothrace, and the next day we went on to Neapolis. From there we travelled to Philippi, a Roman colony and the leading city of that district of Macedonia. And we stayed there several days.

On the Sabbath we went outside the city gate to the river, where we expected to find a place of prayer. We sat down and began to speak to the women who had gathered there. One of those listening was a woman from the city of Thyatira named Lydia, a dealer in purple cloth. She was a worshiper of God. The Lord opened her heart to respond to Paul's message. When she and the members of her household were baptized, she invited us to her home. 'If you consider me a believer in the Lord,' she said, 'come and stay at my house.' And she persuaded us.

Lydia and Paul: Open Doors

Paul's calling to take the gospel to the Gentiles reached a new phase when he crossed the sea from Asia Minor into what we now call Europe. His first journey had brought much joy, but also opposition and suffering. So where next? Doubtless he and his companions spent much time in prayer over this. Guidance comes in various ways: at first they experienced a mysterious series of closed doors – and then a night vision beckoned them across the sea to Macedonia. Imagine the expectation – but perhaps also the trepidation – as they boarded the ship. Clear guidance, or coincidence? Had they discerned rightly?

There was no synagogue at Philippi, so they set out on the Sabbath to find praying people – Jews, converts, seekers after God. Lydia came that morning with other like-minded women to pray by the riverside, and God opened her heart to hear the gospel. Paul's open door became Lydia's open door, not only into her heart but also into her house. The Spirit of God had led the missionaries to a meeting with a woman of means, influence and generosity. Imagine the response among her circle of friends. Imagine the rejoicing at her baptism.

Imagine Paul's thankfulness to God, that out of his journey of faith across the sea, one more journey of faith had started that would see God's Word spread like wildfire across the world.

Lord, give me discernment as I seek your way for me, expectation that you will open the right doors at the right time, and courage to walk through them. Amen.

Amos 7.10–15

Then Amaziah the priest of Bethel sent a message to Jeroboam
king of Israel: 'Amos is raising a conspiracy against you in the
very heart of Israel. The land cannot bear all his words. For
this is what Amos is saying:

"Jeroboam will die by the sword,
and Israel will surely go into exile,
away from their native land."'

Then Amaziah said to Amos, 'Get out, you seer! Go back to
the land of Judah. Earn your bread there and do your prophesying there. Don't prophesy anymore at Bethel, because this
is the king's sanctuary and the temple of the kingdom.'

Amos answered Amaziah, 'I was neither a prophet nor the
disciple of a prophet, but I was a shepherd, and I also took care
of sycamore-fig trees. But the LORD took me from tending the
flock and said to me, "Go, prophesy to my people Israel."'

Amos, Jeroboam and Amaziah: Standing Firm for God

In my dreams I have the courage of Amos, standing firm against the tyrants of this world, upholding the justice of God in the face of intense opposition. In reality, I'm a coward, and often miss the opportunity to speak out. I've always admired people like Amos, who are resolute against conspiracy in high places, no matter what it costs.

We are not told, however, that Amos is brave, or a king-breaker. What Amaziah expected was a logical sequence of events: a prophetic interloper with no backing prophesies doom to the nation, he is reported by the king's spies, and the king is offended. The king instructs his priest to send the prophet back to his own land: he can prophesy there for all that Amaziah cares, so long as he troubles Israel no more.

What actually happened was that Amaziah and Jeroboam were outflanked by an insignificant nobody, who played by no one's rules except God's. Amos had been minding his own business as a shepherd and husbandman, until he was summoned and sent by God. With remarkable simplicity, when presented with a choice between the king's plan and God's plan, he chose God's, assuming that there really was no choice at all.

It's in the naïve assumption that God is sovereign that Amos's strength lies. Courage for the Christian comes not from some inner strength, even if fed by the Holy Spirit. True courage comes from faithful obedience, come what may.

Lord God, give me the faithfulness of Amos, who though he was nobody, spoke against evil in your name, because he knew that he had no choice, and trusted you for strength and courage. Amen.

Mark 15.33–37

At noon, darkness came over the whole land until three in the afternoon. And at three in the afternoon Jesus cried out in a loud voice, *'Eloi, Eloi, lema sabachthani?'* (which means 'My God, my God, why have you forsaken me?').

When some of those standing near heard this, they said, 'Listen, he's calling Elijah.'

Someone ran, filled a sponge with wine vinegar, put it on a staff, and offered it to Jesus to drink. 'Now leave him alone. Let's see if Elijah comes to take him down,' he said.

With a loud cry, Jesus breathed his last.

Jesus Alone: Utter Abandonment

Many have asked down the ages how Christians can believe in a God of love when there is so much pain and suffering in the world. As we stand at the foot of the cross, and hear the first of Jesus' recorded seven words, we are given a clue towards the answer.

Imagine the scene. You are there, at Jesus' crucifixion. It is the middle of the day, but suddenly the sky goes completely dark, as if it were night. You stand in the darkness for three hours, in complete confusion. Suddenly Jesus cries out a cry of agony, the like of which you've never heard before, sending chills down your spine. You don't understand what he says, but you think he's calling for the prophet Elijah. Someone offers Jesus a sponge soaked in vinegar. You all wait for Elijah to miraculously turn up to rescue Jesus. Instead, Jesus cries out again, breathes his last and dies. How do you respond? Should you be relieved that Jesus is dead and his suffering over? Or disappointed that Elijah didn't rescue him? What was that cry to God anyway?

It is that cry of Jesus, coming from his sense of utter abandonment by his Father, that gives us a way to make sense of our suffering. If Jesus can cry out to God, then, surely, we can too. When we are honest with God about our pain he is able to step in, even if, at first, it is only with an infinitesimal glimmer of light.

Lord, you know what it is to feel abandoned, alone and in pain. When I, or those I love, feel abandoned, alone and in pain, help me to cry out to you, trusting that you will hear me and give me a flicker of light in my darkness. Amen.

Luke 23.32–38

Two other men, both criminals, were also led out with him to be executed. When they came to the place called the Skull, they crucified him there, along with the criminals—one on his right, the other on his left. Jesus said, 'Father, forgive them, for they do not know what they are doing.' And they divided up his clothes by casting lots.

The people stood watching, and the rulers even sneered at him. They said, 'He saved others; let him save himself if he is God's Messiah, the Chosen One.'

The soldiers also came up and mocked him. They offered him wine vinegar and said, 'If you are the king of the Jews, save yourself.'

There was a written notice above him, which read: THIS IS THE KING OF THE JEWS.

Jesus and the Penitent Thief: Crazy Forgiveness

What do we do when we have been hurt, misunderstood or contradicted? When we have been wronged, ignored or betrayed? When we encounter the source of this pain, what do we do?

Jesus experienced all this and more. He was left hanging from a piece of wood by rough nails, his body drenched with blood, sweat and spit from bystanders. His body was torn and his lungs struggled for air. Yet, he still uttered these incomprehensible words: 'Father, forgive them, for they do not know what they are doing.'

My heart misses a beat every time I read Jesus' response to those who crucified him, because I know these words of forgiveness are for me also. I have often been an executioner, ignorant and foolish, putting nails into the life around me. Even so, I know that Jesus looks at me, wipes away my tears and says those beautiful, bittersweet words, 'I forgive you.'

My heart also misses a beat because Jesus challenges me to be like him. Jesus invites me to be different from the rest of the world, to leave behind my hatred, anger and desire for revenge and say those wild and grace-filled words, 'Father, forgive them.' Sometimes I can shout it from the roof-tops; at other times I squeeze it through clenched teeth. Always, though, the challenge is to hear Christ gently whispering in my ear, 'I forgive you.'

Father, make me humble enough to receive your forgiveness, and powerful enough to want others to be forgiven. Amen.

Luke 23.39–43

One of the criminals who hung there hurled insults at him: 'Aren't you the Messiah? Save yourself and us!'

But the other criminal rebuked him. 'Don't you fear God,' he said, 'since you are under the same sentence? We are punished justly, for we are getting what our deeds deserve. But this man has done nothing wrong.'

Then he said, 'Jesus, remember me when you come into your kingdom.'

Jesus answered him, 'Truly I tell you, today you will be with me in paradise.'

Two Criminals: The Final Conversation

Talk about a last ditch rescue! Here is drama to eclipse Jonny Wilkinson's final-second drop-goal. The eruption of euphoria at Sydney's Olympic Stadium that followed his World Cup winning kick in 2003 pales into insignificance compared to the party in Heaven over the repentant criminal's final conversation.

As a youth worker, I once had to deal with three teenagers who had stolen and drunk a bottle of vodka on a summer camp. It became obvious that although all were in the wrong, one boy simply could not face what he had done. Avoiding any sense of responsibility, he cast himself as the victim, and hid behind the others. The others knew they were guilty and showed that they were sorry about their crime. They knew the punishment coming to them was deserved. I don't think it is a coincidence that hours later the two sorry teenagers on hearing the message of God's forgiveness, decided to become Christians. But it was impossible to confront the third teenager with God's forgiveness since he had no sense of being in need of it.

Much of the time I too avoid facing up to the deep trouble that I am in. Cloaked behind a façade of respectability, I become an expert at hiding the dark shadows of my heart. Like the unrepentant criminal, I blame everyone else, never reflecting on the blame that I deserve. The repentant criminal teaches us that it is only through being honest with God that, despite our mess, we experience the most radical, unjust grace which invites life-long sinners into his Heavenly Kingdom.

Help me, Lord, to abandon my façade of respectability and to approach you empty handed, admitting my need for forgiveness and my dependence on you. Amen.

Luke 23.44–49

It was now about noon, and darkness came over the whole land until three in the afternoon, for the sun stopped shining. And the curtain of the temple was torn in two. Jesus called out with a loud voice, 'Father, into your hands I commit my spirit.' When he had said this, he breathed his last.

The centurion, seeing what had happened, praised God and said, 'Surely this was a righteous man.' When all the people who had gathered to witness this sight saw what took place, they beat their breasts and went away. But all those who knew him, including the women who had followed him from Galilee, stood at a distance, watching these things.

Jesus and his Father: Ever-present Faithfulness

The focal point of all history, the moment that all that came before had built up to, and all that was to follow would be defined by. Death defeated, a sinful world redeemed, eternal master plan of an eternally loving God nearing its climax. And only with the final words of the dying Saviour did the onlookers realize the magnitude of the event they had just witnessed – the faithfulness of the Father summed up by the simple, final submission of the spirit of the Son.

For Jesus, death on the cross was a cup that had been accepted by choice, in full knowledge of the agonizing suffering that lay ahead. Earlier that day, on a different Jerusalem hillside, blood-like beads of sweat had flowed amidst his supplication to God, earnestly praying that the way of sacrifice be averted. But Jesus knew that his mission would not be fulfilled in any other way, and even as he begged his Father for a way out, he submitted to His will: ' . . . yet, not my will but yours be done.'

Luke tells us that Jesus was abandoned by his disciples that night on the Mount of Olives, both to the exhaustion of grief and, later, the temptation of a warm fire. But where human frailty falls short, heavenly faithfulness triumphs – the ever-present and never-forsaking one was there when it mattered, sending an angel to Jesus at his lowest ebb. It gave him the strength to become the Lamb of God, bearing the cost of every sin that has and ever will be committed.

Father God, I thank you that you are with me always and your faithfulness knows no bounds. Sustain me and equip me for your service today so that I may declare the words of Paul: 'I can do everything through him who gives me strength.' Amen.

John 19.25–27

Near the cross of Jesus stood his mother, his mother's sister, Mary the wife of Clopas, and Mary Magdalene. When Jesus saw his mother there, and the disciple whom he loved standing nearby, he said to her, 'Woman, here is your son,' and to the disciple, 'Here is your mother.' From that time on, this disciple took her into his home.

Mary and John: The Gift of Family

This is a passage of perspectives, human and divine. In the oppressive heat, the Son of God sacrifices himself for all of history and a son watches his mother watching him die.

Mary looks up at the son whom she has nurtured. Perhaps she recalls the words of Simeon at Jesus' dedication: 'A sword will pierce your own soul.' Perhaps she wonders at God's plan. Perhaps she too wants to join in with the crowd as they call on Jesus to 'come down from the cross'.

At the height of Mary's pain and in the midst of his own suffering, Jesus reaches out: 'Woman, here is your son.' With the weight of the world on his shoulders, Jesus calls two of his most precious people into a relationship of support and love.

I always wonder what Mary's response would have been. Could she, like Jesus, see the bigger picture? Did she look at Jesus and think 'But I don't want another son. I want you?'

In times of suffering, confusion and hurt, we may not always get the answer that we want from God. However, we are called to trust in God's provision, even when it seems impossible. God can see every perspective; the intimate details of our lives are as important to him as the big picture of his world.

Lord Jesus, thank you that you know me completely. Help me to trust in your goodness and your provision, even in the most impossible and darkest times. Amen.

John 19.28–30

Later, knowing that everything had now been finished, and so that Scripture would be fulfilled, Jesus said, 'I am thirsty.' A jar of wine vinegar was there, so they soaked a sponge in it, put the sponge on a stalk of the hyssop plant, and lifted it to Jesus' lips. When he had received the drink, Jesus said, 'It is finished.' With that, he bowed his head and gave up his spirit.

Jesus: Encountering Death

One of the first hymns I learned was about that green hill far away, and one line indelibly carved on my mind was that 'he hung and suffered there'. John tells us exactly what that was like, as in searing agony Jesus' earthly life ebbed away. As death envelops, burning him up, he gasps for something to quench the inner fires, if only for a moment. We miss the point of the crucifixion if we separate Christ's dying from the physical consequences of his hideous execution.

And then it is over. Yet as his poor wounded head slumped, he croaked out these last few words, 'It is finished.' Death has finally beaten him. In one dreadful instant he is separated not only from life but from his Father in heaven: no wonder the sky turned black. In that moment he experienced the whole weight and burden of the rebelliousness that wrenches us from a loving Father's arms. Sin is ugly and Jesus bore the consequences of our ugliness.

Yet those last words are ambiguous. All hell rejoiced that the Son of God was vanquished, and then came their sickening realization that far from being a cry of despair, 'It is finished' was in fact the exclamation of victory: 'Job done!' Jesus by dying for us had ultimately defeated death, pulling its sting and opening the Kingdom of Heaven to all believers.

'We may not know, we cannot tell, what pain he had to bear, but we believe it was for us he hung and suffered there.'

Thanks be to you, my Lord Jesus Christ,
For all the benefits you have won for me,
For all the pains and insults you have borne for me.

O most merciful Redeemer, Friend, and Brother,
May I know you more clearly,
Love you more dearly,
And follow you more nearly:
Day by day.

Matthew 27.50–56

And when Jesus had cried out again in a loud voice, he gave up his spirit.

At that moment the curtain of the temple was torn in two from top to bottom. The earth shook, the rocks split and the tombs broke open. The bodies of many holy people who had died were raised to life. They came out of the tombs after Jesus' resurrection and went into the holy city and appeared to many people.

When the centurion and those with him who were guarding Jesus saw the earthquake and all that had happened, they were terrified, and exclaimed, 'Surely he was the Son of God!'

Many women were there, watching from a distance. They had followed Jesus from Galilee to care for his needs. Among them were Mary Magdalene, Mary the mother of James and Joseph, and the mother of Zebedee's sons.

The Centurion: From Onlooker to Believer?

John's report of the last words of Jesus conveys a sense of ful-filment and completion, a divine plan brought to conclusion. In stark contrast, Matthew paints a picture of cosmic shaking, a world falling down in terror, temple boundaries torn apart as the old order gives violent way to the new.

In the chaos, it's easy to miss the onlookers, the women who are there because they loved Jesus, and the soldiers who are there because duty demands they keep watch over the body of a dead man.

And then there's the centurion, celebrated in legend as St Longinus, converted – it is said – into a disciple of Christ. The truth is that we know nothing more than Matthew gives us here, reported for our sake. Even untutored, reluctant sol-diers on duty could tell that on that particular Friday, they had come face to face with the presence and the power of God. They would remember it for the rest of their lives. If they, in their foolishness, fear or slowly dawning awareness of some greater reality, could cry out that they had seen 'a son of God' (which may well have been their words), how much more can we – who know this story from the other side of the grave – cry out in faithful amazement that the world was shaken on Good Friday because THE Son of God had given his life for the life of the world?

Lord Jesus Christ, you were in the form of God, but willingly emptied yourself and embraced death on the cross. Help me to respond to your death not only with amazement but with faith, and with joy that my sins are forgiven and you have vanquished death. Amen.

John 20.11–18

Now Mary stood outside the tomb crying. As she wept, she bent over to look into the tomb and saw two angels in white, seated where Jesus' body had been, one at the head and the other at the foot.

They asked her, 'Woman, why are you crying?'

'They have taken my Lord away,' she said, 'and I don't know where they have put him.' At this, she turned around and saw Jesus standing there, but she did not realize that it was Jesus.

He asked her, 'Woman, why are you crying? Who is it you are looking for?'

Thinking he was the gardener, she said, 'Sir, if you have carried him away, tell me where you have put him, and I will get him.'

Jesus said to her, 'Mary.'

She turned toward him and cried out in Aramaic, 'Rabboni!' (which means 'Teacher').

Jesus said, 'Do not hold on to me, for I have not yet ascended to the Father. Go instead to my brothers and tell them, "I am ascending to my Father and your Father, to my God and your God."'

Mary Magdalene went to the disciples with the news: 'I have seen the Lord!' And she told them that he had said these things to her.

Mary Magdalene and Jesus: Questions of Magnitude

Standing on a chilly train station I watched flabbergasted as a husband summoned his wife with a whistle and a jab of the head to sit down by him when the adjacent seat became vacant. She responded. No doubt she was proficient in translating whistling into English.

This sad episode lingered in my mind as I later read this passage. I was moved to tears by the contrast; Jesus reached out to Mary not by whistling or calling, not with coldness or indifference, but with warmth, tenderness and love, asking: 'Why are you crying? Who is it you are looking for?'

Jesus knows the answers, yet he wants to draw Mary into a conversation – he wants to hear her voice, to hear her answers, to see her searching her heart, to see her finding her Lord. Jesus could have said to Mary, 'Here I am', or 'Stop crying'. But instead he asks the questions that get to the root of the matter.

Jesus knows exactly what needs to be asked to draw out the truth. He asks *us* exactly the same questions, valuing us enough to draw us into a conversation with him, allowing us to look deeper within. It is then that we can look up and recognize that the treasure of our search is standing before our very eyes. And it is only then that Christ can send us out to help others find the true answers to those questions of life and death.

Dear Jesus, help me to hear your gentle voice inviting me into conversation with you. Teach me not to be afraid of what I might find, but to rejoice in your care, your compassion for me and your love. Amen.

John 20.19–23

On the evening of that first day of the week, when the disciples were together, with the doors locked for fear of the Jewish leaders, Jesus came and stood among them and said, 'Peace be with you!' After he said this, he showed them his hands and side. The disciples were overjoyed when they saw the Lord.

Again Jesus said, 'Peace be with you! As the Father has sent me, I am sending you.'

And with that he breathed on them and said, 'Receive the Holy Spirit. If you forgive the sins of anyone, their sins are forgiven; if you do not forgive them, they are not forgiven.'

Jesus and the Disciples: The Other Side of Death

They didn't quite believe Mary Magdalene, did they? She told them that Jesus had found her in the garden, talked to her, re-assured her. Yet here they are, mourning their Master's death, fearful of the Temple authorities, perhaps confused by strange rumours. The solution: to pull up the drawbridge and defend themselves to the death.

Thank God that Jesus doesn't stand on ceremony, then! If they won't open the door, he will ignore it. This is no gentle counselling programme. Fear meets its nemesis as Jesus himself, in the flesh, breathes the Holy Spirit on his friends, bringing new life.

And so fear fades and the drawbridge falls down. In the face of death's defeat, everything changes for the disciples. This new meeting with Jesus is like no other; their joy is the joy of knowing that he will be with them and for them, forever. No farewell this, but the beginning of a new relationship in which Jesus is always present through his Spirit. They will never have to worry about losing him again: he is with them – and us – until the end of the age.

Even more, through his Spirit in them – and in us – Jesus will continue to walk the earth, changing lives, forgiving sinners, giving good news to the poor, proclaiming release to the captives, sight to the blind, and letting the oppressed go free. This is indeed the year of the Lord's favour.

Heavenly Father, I rejoice that you have raised Jesus Christ from death, and that through his Spirit he is still with me now. May all who meet me encounter him, discover that joy, and turn to follow him away from fear, into the freedom of a new life. Amen.

The Editors and Contributors

THE EDITORS

Adrian Chatfield

Jill Chatfield

Richard Gilbert

Katy Holbird

Ali Walton

Kathryn Wehr

Natasha Wilkinson

Steve Wilkinson

THE CONTRIBUTORS

Charlie Boyle

Sarah Boyle

Dave Britton

Jan Bunday

Adrian Chatfield

Jill Chatfield

Andy Cranston

Toby Crowe

Ian Dyble

Jaiye Edu

David Frederick

Rebecca Gilbert

Richard Gilbert

Hannah Haigh

Sam Haigh

Annette Hawkins

Katy Holbird

Tom Holbird

Philip Jenson

Claire Johnson

Emma Johnson

Jane Keiller

Richard Kew

Rosemary Kew

Will Leaf

Chris Lee

Rachel Livesey

David Lloyd

Derek McClean

Elisheva Mechanic

Jez Safford

Mark Smith

Mike Terry

Mike Thompson

Gill Toogood

About Ridley Hall

When Ridley Hall first opened its doors in Cambridge in the 1880s even the wildest optimist could not have predicted the impact the college would have for Jesus Christ in Britain and around the world. In our chapel are memorials remembering all those Ridleians who gave their lives in obedience to the Great Commission of Jesus Christ.

Throughout those years, Ridley Hall has continually been renewing itself, and today not only forms men and women for ordination in the Church of England and the worldwide church, but also trains youth leaders, and undertakes a host of other activities to equip lay Christians for their ministry in a rapidly changing culture.

To find out a lot more about Ridley and all that we do, please visit our website

www.ridley.cam.ac.uk

If you have appreciated the devotions in this book and would like to know more about Ridley, then please get in touch with us. There's a lot going on that might help you with your own Christian discipleship. It could be that you are interested in praying for or supporting us, or even coming here as a student.

Raising up twenty-first-century leaders to tackle the unique challenges of today requires courage, creativity, and significant resources. We invite you to:

- Pray for Ridley's ministry
- Become a regular donor to Ridley's work
- Make a gift of stocks or shares to Ridley Hall
- Include Ridley in your will
- Encourage others to be part of the wider Ridley community.

If you need help with any of these things or would like more information please contact Ridley Hall's Development Office (development@ridley.cam.ac.uk or call us at 01223 741079).

Ridley Hall is a registered charity (no. 311456) and is a member of the Cambridge Theological Federation.

About The Simeon Centre for Prayer and the Spiritual Life

The Simeon Centre is an initiative of Ridley Hall, with the aim of strengthening the life of prayer. In its mission, it fully reflects the ethos of Ridley: we have our 'roots down' in the evangelical Anglican tradition, and are committed to the centrality of prayer in the life of a mission-shaped church: to the Father, through his Son, in the power of the Holy Spirit.

We also live with 'walls down' in an open, generous and even risky commitment to bringing out of the treasures of Christ's church 'things old and things new', learning from classical and contemporary Christian spiritualities and exploring a wide range of Christian prayer and spiritual disciplines.

Ridley Hall, and the Centre, are missional at heart, and so we have 'bridges out'. Our passion and aim is to help church leaders and congregations around the country, to grow in their desire and capacity to pray, and to equip them to become leaders and teachers who enable others to pray. The same is true for those at Ridley and who are part of the Cambridge Theological Federation.

We are named after the biblical Simeon who, having held the baby Jesus, was content to die, because he had seen the Saviour promised by God. The Centre also honours the famous Cambridge Christian Charles Simeon, Vicar of Holy Trinity for 54 years in the eighteenth century, and a man of deep prayer and spirituality.

As part of our work we:

- offer conferences and quiet days for the wider church;
- are growing a Simeon Community, a dispersed intentional community of prayer living by a simple shared Rule of Life;
- help churches to develop prayer resources and forms of training;
- are exploring the possibility of developing projects in spirituality as evangelism;
- offer opportunities and advice for spiritual direction and sabbaticals.

To find out more about the Centre and all that we do, please visit our website

www.simeoncentre.co.uk

If you are interested the being part of the work of the Centre in any way, sense that God might be calling you to join the Simeon Community, or would like to contribute to it financially, we would be delighted if you would get in touch with us through the website or by email to rak44@cam.ac.uk.

Index of Bible Passages Cited